you are not a lost soul

If you are like most people, you do not fear death itself. You fear the prospect of not being, or rather of unbeing—a state where you cease to exist altogether. The idea of unbeing is so foreign to us that we find it almost impossible to conceive. We do not want to stop experiencing life. We do not want to stop being.

Therefore, it is personality survival that we are concerned with when we think about death and of what may happen after we die. It is our innermost thoughts and feelings—the very essence of our humanity—that we are afraid of losing.

If we were not so afraid of death, if we knew for certain that the personality survives after death, we would be able to face life with a deeper sense of purpose. We would know that our soul is on an evolutionary path. Its course is neither random nor without purpose. We exist now and forever for a reason.

What Happens After Death presents strong scientific and personal evidence for personality survival after death. Migene González-Wippler deftly merges the empirical world of science with the ethereal world of spirit and gives you a fully researched argument for soul survival; but most importantly, she gives you the gift of hope. . . .

about the author

Migene González-Wippler was born in Puerto Rico and has degrees in psychology and anthropology from the University of Puerto Rico and from Columbia University. She has worked as a science editor for the Interscience Division of John Wiley, the American Institute of Physics, and the American Museum of Natural History, and as an English editor for the United Nations in Vienna, where she lived for many years. She is a cultural anthropologist and lectures frequently at universities and other educational institutions. She is the noted author of many books on religion and mysticism, including the widely acclaimed *Santería: African Magic in Latin America, The Complete Book of Spells, Ceremonies & Magic,* and *Dreams and What They Mean to You.*

how to write to the author

If you wish to contact the author or would like more information about this book, please write to the author in care of Llewellyn Worldwide, and we will forward your request. Both the author and publisher appreciate hearing from you and learning of your enjoyment of this book and how it has helped you. Llewellyn Worldwide cannot guarantee that every letter written to the author can be answered, but all will be forwarded. Please write to:

Migene González-Wippler
℅ Llewellyn Worldwide
P.O. Box 64383, Dept. K327-1
St. Paul, MN 55164-0383, U.S.A.

Please enclose a self-addressed stamped envelope for reply, or $1.00 to cover costs. If outside U.S.A., enclose international postal reply coupon.

MIGENE GONZÁLEZ-WIPPLER

International Bestseller

WHAT HAPPENS AFTER DEATH

Scientific & Personal Evidence for Survival

1997
Llewellyn Publications
St. Paul, Minnesota 55164-0383

FIRST EDITION
First Printing, 1997

Cover Design by Tom Grewe
Cover Art from Digital Stock Photography
Editing and Book Design by Rebecca Zins

Library of Congress Cataloging-in-Publication Data

González-Wippler, Migene.
    What happens after death: scientific & personal
evidence for survival / Migene González-Wippler.—1st ed.
        p. cm.
    Includes bibliographical references and index.
    ISBN 1-56718-327-1 (trade paper)
    1. Future life. 2. Parapsychology. 3. Occultism. I. Title.
  BL535.G663   1997
  133.9'01'3—dc21   97–1983
                                                              CIP

Llewellyn Publications
A Division of Llewellyn Worldwide, Ltd.
P.O. Box 64383, Dept. K327-1
St. Paul, MN 55164-0383, U.S.A.

*This book is lovingly dedicated to
my mother, and to Fide, Nikolas,
Christopher, Fernando, John, Herman,
Ivar, Mike, Eduardo, Pancho,
Lillian, Willie, and all the others
who have preceded me into the Light,
until we meet again.*

§

other books by migene gonzález-wippler

Santería: African Magic in Latin America
Rituals and Spells of Santería
The Seashells

available from llewellyn publications

The Complete Book of Amulets and Talismans
The Complete Book of Spells, Ceremonies & Magic
Dreams and What They Mean to You
A Kabbalah for the Modern World
Legends of Santería
La Magia de Las Piedras y Los Cristales (in Spanish)
La Magia y Tu (in Spanish)
Peregrinaje (in Spanish)
Santería: The Religion
The Santería Experience
Sueños (in Spanish)

contents

acknowledgments

EVERY BOOK IS THE RESULT of the efforts of many people other than its author. And so it is with this one. I wish I could thank individually each person who helped make this book possible. Unfortunately, I have been informed by my editor that I have very little space in which to express my gratitude to everyone concerned. I can only thank them in my heart and in my prayers, for many of them are no longer in the world of matter. They are, however, in the world of spirit, and I know they are aware of my love and gratitude.

That leaves those who are in the physical world, and they are also many. Among them I would like to thank specially Carl and Sandra Weschcke of Llewellyn, who shared my vision when this book was first conceived. The book was originally written in Spanish, and it took a great deal of courage to publish it when they could not read it. I thank them for their trust in my work and for their belief in the message that the book conveyed. I am also deeply indebted to Professor Ernst Senkowski of Mainz, Germany, and his wife, Adelhaide, for their invaluable contribution on the subject of Instrumental Transcommunication (ITC), which makes up chapter 2 of the book. Without their generosity and wisdom, that valuable information could not have been included here. My gratitude also to Brenda J. Dunne and Professor Robert J. Jahn of the PEAR lab at Princeton University for the valuable information on the quantum mechanics of consciousness. None of this would have been possible without the generous cooperation of TV correspondent Michele Marsh, who made her sources on ITC available to me. Many thanks to her also and to my editor at Llewellyn, Rebecca Zins, whose valuable advice helped shape up the translation.

My special thanks to the readers who made the Spanish version a success, and the English version a reality, and to the new readers who are still to read the book, for their interest in this work. I hope the message within will find echoes in their souls.

preface

ONE OF OUR MOST PREVALENT obsessions is the fragility of the human body and the inescapable reality that one day it will die. What happens after the unavoidable trauma of death? Do we continue to exist in another unknown and invisible world? When we exhale our last breath, do we—our personalities, our minds, and the other things that we are—cease to exist? And what about those who have gone before us to that mysterious "other" world? Will we meet them again? Will we resume relationships, friendships, and loves that were part of our lives and somehow left their indelible marks forever in our souls?

To find answers to these questions, which are really only one question fragmented into a thousand echoes, we have built great schools of philosophy, formulated profound theological concepts, and produced sublime literary works. Both science and religion have delved deeply into the great Unknown and have come up with a vast array of possible answers, all of them equally uncertain.

What is it that we have learned through almost two million years of existence on this planet? What does science tell us about life after death? How do the different religions explain the mystery? What is the answer given by the strange mystical science known as Spiritism?

How much credibility can we give to Spiritism's spiritual concepts? These and other questions about life after death will be explored in this book.

It is not easy to maintain an objective attitude with a topic as subjective as the survival of the personality after death, but I have endeavored to present all the relevant information as impartially as possible. The various studies and scientific discoveries mentioned in the book are of general topical relevance, and all can be verified easily.

The first part of the book is an objective study of life after death. The second part is a subjective presentation of the experiences of a spiritual being through his various incarnations, what he calls a pilgrimage. The two sections are so different from each other that they could almost be considered two separate books. In reality, they are simply expressing the same concepts in different ways.

It is not my intention to present the reader a rigid or dogmatic view of life after death. With a topic as intangible as this one, it is almost impossible to establish a dogma. I have tried to do an in-depth exploration of the topic using simple scientific concepts, most of which we learned in elementary school, as well as relevant mystical and spiritual beliefs.

There is little new in this book, mostly new ways of presenting and adapting old concepts. Astute readers will claim that there is also scientific evidence supporting the theory that after death, there is nothing at all. This theory is as valid as my own. All I want to demonstrate is that there is enough scientific and nonscientific evidence to support the idea that life after death is not only possible but also quite probable. And, as Aristotle has shown us with great wit, the probable is what usually happens.

In the course of this book, I will present to the reader not only a series of fascinating concepts but also a character, equally fascinating, who jointly will attempt to show you what probably happens after we die.

after death

what happens

what happens

after death

part one: theories

after death

what happens

after we die: a theory

what happens

after death

1 THE PROBLEM WITH THE IDEA

of dying is that most people are so afraid of death that they do not even want to discuss it. It is one of those topics one talks about in whispers and with the utmost reluctance. We would rather forget about the distasteful subject altogether and concentrate on living life to the fullest, pursuing its many pleasures with the most devoted concentration. Ignoring the gloomy perspective of our unwelcome demise will not make it go away. From time to time, especially when we are faced with a personal crisis, the thought of death rears its ugly head, and we are again forced to consider the inevitable moment, our minds numbed with fear.

What we fear most is not death itself but the prospect of not being, or rather of *unbeing*, a state where we altogether cease to exist. The idea of unbeing is so alien to us that we find it almost impossible to conceive. The reason for this inability to face the end of life is that we are so immersed in our own sense of awareness that we cannot bear the idea of losing it forever. It is not so much that we do not want to leave this life, but rather that we do not want to stop experiencing it. We do not want to stop being.

Many human tragedies and sorrows could have been averted if we were not so afraid of dying, if we did not feel so hopeless about the idea of unbeing. In many cases it is far less traumatic and painful for us to think of the end of

3

our own awareness than it is to think of the end of another deeply cherished and most-beloved person. There is an inexpressible, soul-rending pain in the loss of a loved one that is unlike any other pain we experience as human beings. There is no comfort to be had at that time. No religious belief and no words of kindness can soothe or drive away the terrible sense of utter desolation and despair. The reason for the despair and desolation is the feeling that this person is irretrievably lost to us, that his or her personality has ceased to be, that we cannot hope to share love or joy or even pain with him or her ever again. Religion may give us hope for a future life in a much better world, but at the moment of death, our deepest religious convictions are tried to the utmost and often rejected in anger and resentment.

Therefore, it is personality survival that we are concerned with when we think about death and of what may happen after we die. It is our innermost thoughts and feelings, the very essence of our humanity, that we are afraid of losing. We are so afraid to lose them, and so sure we inevitably will, that our frantic existences are concentrated on the pursuit of life's pleasures while ignoring the most important moment of our lives: the time when we will be embarking on the most awesome of all adventures.

If we were not so afraid of death, if we knew without any doubt that we go on living after the death of the physical body, if we knew for certain that the conscious personality survives and the mind continues to be, we would be able to face life with a deeper sense of purpose, with gratitude and joy for the great gift of living. We would lose all sense of despair and misery at the loss of a loved one because we would know that we would indeed meet them again in another wondrous world. We would see other human beings with a sense of love and unification and learn to enjoy life with more excitement and commitment than ever before.

Above all, we would prepare for that final voyage by being better people, by accepting the experiences of life—both positive and negative—as fulfilling and enriching the growth of our spiritual and personal awareness. We would be gaining the greatest gift of all: the gift of hope.

Interestingly enough, there is a great deal of scientific data sustaining the notion that our awareness, as well as our personality, survives the trauma of death. Many scientists are convinced this is indeed the case but are hesitant to express their views because of lack of empirical proof. The very nature of science demands proof for every theory and postulate; for a scientist to make a statement about life after death that is unsubstantiated by verifiable and replicable experimentation is to endanger both name and reputation. This is why we must find the scientific evidence ourselves, examine it, and piece it together to form a cohesive and weighty case for personality survival. Among the most powerful arguments supporting the concept of life after death are the laws of nature.

One of nature's basic laws is the first law of thermodynamics, which states that energy can neither be created nor destroyed. Its form can be changed by physical or chemical processes, but its essence can never be altered. On the other hand, matter is anything that possesses mass and occupies space. It is also a form of energy. A simple example of matter is paper. According to the first law of thermodynamics, if a paper is cut into several pieces, each piece is still paper, even though there is a physical change in the matter that we call paper. If the paper is burned instead of cut, its matter is transformed by the chemical process of combustion, which divides the paper into different atoms. These particles scatter into the atmosphere, leaving only ashes in our hands, but this does not mean the energy that formed the paper was destroyed. What happened was that the different components of the paper were separated but still exist individually in our surroundings, even though we do not see them. That particular form of matter may not exist as paper, but all the particles that formed the paper still exist. Nothing has been lost. The matter of the paper was not destroyed, only transformed.

These are all simple teachings we learn in elementary school. But it has often been said it is the simple things that hold the answers to our most profound questions. And so it is with the first law of thermodynamics.

When this law states that energy can neither be created nor destroyed, it is referring to the electromagnetic energy that forms the atom and its subatomic particles. The whole universe is based on this radiant electromagnetic energy. The atom itself is made up of three main particles: the proton with a positive electrical charge, the electron with a negative charge, and the neutron with a neutral charge. Both the protons and the neutrons are in the nucleus, while the electrons revolve in tiny orbits around the nucleus. The number of electrons and protons that form an atom are always equal and are what determine the various elements and the different manifestations of energy that are known as matter. Recently science has discovered new elementary particles, such as quarks, and the possibility is now beginning to emerge that all forms of matter may consist of a small number of these particles.

The simplest element is hydrogen, with only one proton and one electron. The element oxygen has eight protons and eight electrons in its atom. Two hydrogen atoms and one oxygen atom give us a visible form of matter that we all know as water. If water is heated to a boil, its atoms become separated through the process of evaporation, and the liquid is transformed into vapor. Although the physical qualities of the water are different, the atoms that formed it still exist even though we don't see them. Eventually some of them will reunite through the process of condensation and become the phenomenon we know as rain. This is what the first law of thermodynamics wants to express when it says that energy cannot be created or destroyed. In other words, nothing is new in the Universe. What we are constantly seeing are different formations of the same atoms, which separate and regroup through different physical, chemical, and biochemical processes.

§

At this point you are probably asking: What does this have to do with life after death? In this chapter, we want to establish a theory about what happens after we die. In order to do this, we must first provide a foundation for this theory, and this foundation is the first law of thermodynamics. So far we have seen that this law states that energy can neither be created nor destroyed. How does this affect the death phenomenon? Before we attempt to answer this question, we should look into what science tells us about the human mind.

As we stated previously, everything that has matter, or mass, is formed by atoms, which are a form of electromagnetic energy. Our brain is constantly producing this kind of energy. How do we know? Because there is a machine called the electroencephalograph that neurologists use to measure electrical activity in the brain.

Neurologists know if an electrode is connected to each side of the head, the resulting energy produced by mental activity can light a five-watt bulb. This tells us the brain is emitting electromagnetic waves of great intensity as long as a person lives. This electrical activity is related to what we call thought and the activities of the human mind. When a person dies, the electroencephalograph stops registering electrical activity in the brain.

If neurology is the science that studies the brain and the nervous system, psychology is the science that studies the thought processes. Neurology can explain the distinct processes by which the brain and nervous system work, but it cannot explain why we think, nor can it explain the extraordinary phenomenon that is the mind. These explanations come from the world of psychology.

Although modern psychology has taken great steps toward understanding the human psyche, it is still a long way from knowing exactly what the mind is. Many neurologists and psychologists have begun to suspect that the mind is not really part of the brain, based on the fact that nobody has been able to locate the mind or to explain the phenomenon of thought in any of the functions and activities of the brain. It is certain that a link exists between the mind and the brain, but they seem to exist separately from each other. What we do know is that thought is electromagnetic in nature because mental activity can be measured electronically.

We have all heard many accounts about the phenomena of telepathy and clairvoyance. Most human beings have had several experiences of this type in their lifetime. Almost everybody has had the experience of thinking about someone and then "accidentally" meeting that person in the street or getting a telephone call from them. There are also premonitory dreams, in which we clearly see a specific event that occurs shortly afterward.

Swiss psychoanalyst Carl Gustav Jung theorized that the combined unconscious minds of all of humanity form a great lake, which he called the collective unconscious. According to Jung, when people are asleep or drifting into sleep, in what is known as the alpha state, they automatically merge with the collective unconscious, where they may come into contact with other human minds. It is during this time that a person may meet someone he or she knows on an unconscious level and in this way exchange messages or information. This unconscious exchange is one of the explanations given to the phenomena of telepathy or clairvoyance.

When we sleep, our minds are moving in a world formed almost entirely of images from our memories and experiences. This other world can also contain ancestral memories, consisting of the experiences of our forebears, passed on to us genetically through our parents. The world of the mind, often identified with the astral world, is formed of images and symbols. It is a world that is highly visual and in which we are usually spectators. It is also a world in which nothing is as it appears: all or nearly all that happens is symbolic. Many of these symbols are personal and have meaning only for the dreamer. Other symbols are elements, or symbols, that have the same or a similar meaning for all members of the human race.

Nothing that is seen, felt, or done in a dream surprises us while we dream. The most unlikely experiences, the most impossible situations, seem perfectly normal. Extraordinary beings, phantasmagorical figures, strange colors, cataclysmic events, divine or terrifying experiences—all this and more form a natural part of our dream life, a life we accept as readily as the one we experience in the physical world. Sometimes, but not very often, we realize that we are dreaming. This is a state known as the lucid dream. For the most part, we simply accept our nocturnal foray into the astral or mind's world as a very real and natural experience. This world of images where everything is possible and nothing seems strange, the world of pure mind, was known by the ancients as the true world of the spirit.

In his enduring classic *Origin of Species*, Charles Darwin tells us that only the strongest survive in nature. Those that do not adapt, perish. Those who are strong, who adapt, or who are valuable in the natural scheme of life, survive. And we know that through four billion years of evolution, nature has preferred and preserved that which has demonstrated itself to be strong and versatile. Dinosaurs lived for forty million years because they were admirably adapted to the natural world in which they existed at the time. The lowly cockroach is one of the oldest species on Earth. It has survived because it is adaptable and can live anywhere and eat anything. It may not be one of the most appealing species, but it is undoubtedly one of the most successful on the planet.

So far in our search we have established the following facts:

1. The first law of thermodynamics tells us that matter, or electromagnetic energy, can neither be created nor destroyed.

2. Neurology tells us that the brain emits measurable electromagnetic waves that can be used to identify activities associated with the human mind.

3. Many psychologists and neurologists suspect that the electromagnetic field that is the mind, and can be identified as human thought processes, may well function independently of the brain.

4. Jung has taught us that the unconscious part of the mind can communicate with other unconscious minds during sleep or when in an alpha state.

5. The world of the mind, called by many the astral world, is a world of images and symbols where everything is possible and nothing is surprising.

6. This astral world is the world of dreams, where we travel whenever we sleep.

7. For his part, Darwin has shown us that nature preserves all that is strong and valuable.

Based on these simple and well-known data, we can theorize the following:

1. *The human mind is made of electromagnetic energy, and since energy cannot be destroyed, then it follows that the human mind cannot be destroyed either.*

2. *If the mind functions independently of the body, as science suspects, then when the body dies, the mind will continue to exist independently of the body.*

3. *The mind, and the awareness of the personality, will then exist in the astral world that we know as the world of our dreams. This is the world of symbols and images that is the culmination of our experiences and the experiences of our ancestors.*

4. *If nature has seen fit to preserve millions of species for millions of years, it is logical to assume that it should also seek to preserve the human mind and its great creative potential. This is supported by the fact that nature preserves that which is strong and valuable, and the most valuable thing that has ever evolved on this planet is the human mind.*

According to all of this, after we die, the physical body decomposes into its basic elements, which are then recycled by nature to create other life forms. The mind, which is pure electromagnetic energy, once disembodied has no physical substance and continues to exist in the astral world, where it becomes a part of the collective memories and experiences of that world. This is what is called the human spirit, the personality of an individual, and it is how we identify ourselves in the world. While the world of matter passes after we die, the world of mind—our true essence, where we rest each and every night—is the final resting place where our awareness continues to exist after the end of physical life.

In other words, based on what science has to tell us, we can postulate that our personality does survive the trauma of physical death and continues to live in another world or on another spiritual, or astral, plane. But for how long? Can we contact other entities in the spiritual plane? Do angels and spirit guides exist? What is the death experience like? Is there such a thing as evil spirits? What happens to criminals and people who commit suicide? What happens in the astral plane? Are there other worlds or planes? Is there a heaven or a hell? These and other similar questions will be addressed in this book.

Much of what will be presented here has nothing to do with science. It may be labeled speculation, fantasy, imagination, or spiritual insight. It is the human spirit's answer to science's unanswerable questions. Nothing we can imagine, no matter how fantastic, can come close to the spectacular designs of the Universe. In the images transmitted back to Earth from Voyager's trip across the solar system, there are photos of one of the moons of Uranus, called Miranda, that reveal landscapes more fantastic than anything we can find in our science fiction. Golden mountains traversed by gigantic fountains of molten metal soaring thousands of feet into the air stunned astrophysicists. The ten-year

Voyager project uncovered enough startling new information to force us to reexamine all our previous theories about the solar system. Many scientific texts must now be rewritten to include the new data. Also in the last few years, astrophysicists have discovered a dark matter they believe forms about 90 percent of the Universe. Nobody knows what it is made of, but scientists suspect that only about 10 percent of the Universe is visible, the remaining 90 percent being composed of invisible dark matter. It has been speculated that these invisible particles are passing through our bodies all the time, radically altering our lives. What are they? Where are they from? Nobody knows.

There are many things we know nothing about. We do not know how the Universe originated. We do not know what, if anything, existed before it came into being. We do not know all the laws that regulate it. We do not even know if the world as we know it is simply a figment of God's imagination. Compared with these mysteries, the enigma of life after death and our own puny existences seem almost an afterthought.

§

after death

what happens

ghostly voices on the rhine

what happens

after death

2 ON FEBRUARY 8, 1995, CBS AIRED a special entitled *Voices from Beyond*, hosted by then-CBS correspondent Michele Marsh. The three-part special dealt with life after death and presented some very compelling evidence on survival. It included footage of ghostly faces and voices from deceased people allegedly taped in Germany and other European countries through a system known as ITC, or Instrumental Transcommunication.

I was very interested in the program and immediately contacted CBS to get more information about it. Michele Marsh and other members of the CBS personnel were extremely cooperative and made the tapes available to me for a private viewing in their New York offices. Viewing the tapes convinced me that I wanted to do further research on the material presented in them. My idea was to add the information to the book you are now reading, which is the English translation of my original book in Spanish, *Peregrinaje*.

This research included a trip to Germany, where I interviewed two of the principal experimenters on ITC, and upon my return to the United States, a visit to Princeton University, where some fascinating experiments are being conducted on ESP, especially psychokinesis.

I arrived in Germany in mid-April. My destination was the sleepy town of Mainz, about fifteen minutes by train from bustling Frankfurt. As we approached Mainz, the flat, dull landscape changed abruptly, and the quaint spires of medieval churches could be seen in the distance. There was a profusion of flowers everywhere, most of them planted in carefully coordinated designs on perfectly trimmed lawns. The private houses and the taller buildings that could be seen from the train looked expectedly neat and well organized, like most things German. Mainz, I thought to myself, is the sort of place an elderly couple can retire to on a comfortable pension to ensure a life free of the stress and frantic pace of larger cities. I was to meet such a couple soon after my arrival in town.

Prior to my trip, I had exchanged several letters and telephone conversations with one of the leading researchers on Instrumental Transcommunication in Europe. This researcher, Dr. Ernst Senkowski, is an experimental physicist who studied at the University of Hamburg and the University of Mainz, where he received his doctorate in 1958 after building a small electron accelerator. Soon after this, Dr. Senkowski joined UNESCO and was sent to Cairo to teach physics at Cairo University and its laboratory at the National Research Center. He stayed in Egypt for fifteen months and returned to Germany in the beginning of 1960. A friend of his, who was doing research at Bingham on the Rhine, near Mainz, suggested that he should apply for a job as a professor of physics at the University at Bingham. Dr. Senkowski followed up on the suggestion and was appointed to the faculty of physics, where he taught physics and electrotechnical subjects from 1961 until his retirement a few years ago. Now he lives in a pretty cottage on the university campus with his wife, Adelhaide. It was there that he took me after a short drive around Mainz, which he and his charming wife insisted on showing me before we sat down to a late-evening dinner the first day of my stay in Mainz. As we ate, I brought out my small tape recorder, and Ernst began to explain ITC.

§

By definition, Instrumental Transcommunication (ITC) is technically supported contact with beings, entities, or informational structures in realms that normally are inaccessible to our physical senses. The technical devices or instruments used by ITC are audio recorders, radio receivers, telephones, video recorders, televisions, and computers, all of which "behave irregularly" during transcommunications, delivering voices, images, and messages of varying quality, sometimes excellent, coming apparently from nowhere. In transcommunication the researcher is apparently establishing contact with other ranges of consciousness, including the dead. At such times, a border that appears to exist between our world and other, unknown regions seems to be crossed. ITC researchers call such realms of existence *transregions*. When information from such regions is received or exchanged, it is said that a communication has been established. From these two terms, *transregions* and *communication,* was coined the name of this type of research: transcommunication. The word *instrumental* was added to indicate that such communication is received through various instruments or devices.

Voices on tape (VOT) were first documented in the 1950s in the United States, Italy, and Sweden. Video images received through television appeared later. More recently, contact or transcommunication has been made through computers, especially the Commodore 64, which is no longer on the market. It is to be expected that the newer computers will be just as effective in receiving messages from beyond our physical plane.

Ernst was adamant in his assertion that research is not a word he likes to use in relation to ITC. He explained that all the work that is done around the "border sciences," such as ITC, is just study. The reasons why research cannot be done on taped voices or televised images, according to him, are dual. First, there is no definite theory behind ITC because no one knows how these phenomena take place, and second, the results of the investigations being conducted cannot be replicated under laboratory conditions. Replication or duplication is at the core of all scientific research, and therefore any experimentation that cannot be replicated is unrealistic and scientifically unacceptable. ITC and the phenomena it creates are spontaneous and unlikely to be created under laboratory conditions.

This is not to say that scientists are uninterested in the subject of communication with other levels of being. Ernst Senkowski is by no means the first scientist to devote time and effort to the phenomena of communication with the dead or with other worlds. World-famous scientists like Nikola Tesla, Guglielmo Marconi, and Thomas Edison experimented with special devices in the hope of establishing such contacts. Today there are many teams of operators conducting various experiments on ITC in twelve different countries. More than sixty monographs have been published on the subject in seven languages. Ernst and a friend also publish a journal on ITC that has about 400 subscribers from different countries, among which are Brazil and the United States.

At this point in our conversation, our dinner pleasantly concluded, Ernst suggested that he show me examples of taped voices, recorded TV images, and computer messages. I wanted to know first how Ernst became so deeply involved with ITC, and he explained at some length that the first time he learned about the subject, as a scientist he felt it would be interesting to find out if these phenomena really existed. He began by contacting several people who were familiar with ITC to ask their views about the subject. He got mixed reviews. Some people said it was nonsense, and others said it was real. Ernst was very skeptical himself but decided to experiment on his own.

He began with a shortwave radio tuned in to different European stations with a mixture of several languages. Next to the radio he set a tape recorder to tape everything that came through. He used a shortwave radio because in shortwave radios the stations are very close to each other, so one can tune to a spot on the dial where several stations are jammed in together. In this manner, one could presumably distinguish among the many voices speaking all at once—voices that are not of this world. Naturally, from Germany he would get many different countries with a corresponding variety of languages.

The first three or four times he tried, he used medium waves, and the result was such a terrible cacophony of sound he was unable to understand anything. Then he tried short waves and it worked immediately. In fact, it happened so quickly that he was astonished. The voices that came through said they were in another dimension of being, that at one time they had lived on Earth and we would consider them dead, but that they were not dead, only existing in another plane. Then Ernst's father came through, then an uncle and an old friend. An interesting comment Ernst made was that as soon as one of these disembodied voices came through, all the other voices of living human beings on the radio were automatically lowered so that the voice from the other side was quite clear and easy to understand.

When Ernst's father came through the short waves, he spoke in his native Prussian dialect and addressed Ernst with the name he used to call him when Ernst was a small boy. This name, *pomuckel,* means "little elf"—a suitable epithet as Ernst still has an elfish quality about him, a permanent grin lighting up his face and his small, twinkling eyes. This experience with his father left Ernst badly shaken. As hard as he tried, he could not find a logical explanation for the transmission. The voice could only come from his father because no one else knew about this family nickname, yet his father had been dead for many years. This particular experience and the others that followed convinced Ernst that the ITC phenomena were real.

After these experiences, Ernst tried to improve the radio transmissions with more advanced technology but was unable to do so. He began reading some of the literature available on ITC and learned that the best transmissions come through people who are naturally psychic, with a special talent for this type of transcommunication with other levels of existence. In other words, according to ITC experimentation, not all psychic people are able to establish contact with outside entities. One specific problem that plagues the people engaged in this type of experiment is the voices that come through are only on the air for less than two seconds. This makes prolonged communication or a series of questions and answers nearly impossible to achieve.

After experimenting with shortwave radio for several years, Ernst decided to contact other people who were doing the same kind of work. He found several in Germany, England, Austria, Italy, and Luxembourg. They all reported that the speech used by these entities was not a normal type of speech but somehow slower and in some instances garbled. This made it easy to distinguish the ITC transmissions from the average radio sounds. The foremost pioneers on VOT were Friedrich Jurgenson from Sweden and Konstantin Raudive from Germany, although important work was also done by Theodor Rudolph from Germany, Franz Seidl from Austria, and Leo Schmid, a Catholic priest from Switzerland.

I then asked what it was like on the other side. Ernst said that the voices always speak of a world where there exists another kind of logic and different semantics, which make it difficult to communicate in simple, clear terms. In one instance, an entity that came through spoke of another world where everything is malleable and reality can be altered through mental manipulation. In other words, it is possible in this other plane to change one's surroundings simply by willing it mentally. Another voice described our world as a world of shadows and their world as true reality.

After the initial experiences with VOT through shortwave radio, experimenters began to use radio speakers. This was followed by experimentation with video systems, and then the first faces appeared on TV. After this, messages began to appear on computer screens, first a few words, then longer messages.

Ernst then suggested we go up to his study, where he wanted to show me actual photographs and videos where faces of several deceased people, some well known, had appeared on TV accompanied by brief spoken messages. There he demonstrated how actual faces can be taped on television. It is a long and tedious process, often taking many hours and sometimes days. What the experimenter does is set up a constantly running video camera in front of a television set that is tuned to a free channel. The screen will be covered with a fuzzy, crackling image, accompanied by the noise of heavy static. After hours of videotaping the apparently empty screen, the experimenter will sit down patiently to watch the tape run. Most of the time it is an exercise in futility, and nothing is found on the tape. But sometimes an image begins to form in the midst of the fuzzy screen, until it resolves into an actual face. If the experimenter is lucky, the face will be accompanied by a voice not of this world. One of the earlier experimenters, Klaus Schreiber, used this method. He tuned the TV set to a free channel and proceeded to tape the empty screen. Then he went back and enlarged the screen. At first a faint image appeared. He continued to enlarge it until the image was complete. This is done in segments. First you get the impression that a nose is forming, then the eyes appear, and then the chin. You go over this several times until the image is defined.

Ernst showed me a photograph taken off a screen where the image of the late German actress Romy Schneider had appeared. It was not very clear, just a contour, but her features were discernible. It came from a clip of one of her films. During an exercise done in front of a television crew in Luxembourg, the face of Albert Einstein came through on the screen. There was no voice, only the image. The members of the crew were so shaken that they refused to continue the exercise. Similar cases have been reported by other researchers. Ernst explained that there can be no outside interference or tampering with these transmissions because they come through closed-circuit TV. It is against all logic for these images and voices to come through, yet they do.

One of the first faces to appear on a TV screen in this manner was that of Konstantin Raudive, one of the earlier pioneers of VOT. Raudive's face, like all of the faces of deceased people who have appeared on TV screens, is a faint copy of one of the photographs taken of him while he was still alive. I found this rather disconcerting, and I asked Ernst why a photograph of a dead person should appear on screen as he or she apparently tries to establish contact with our world. Why doesn't the actual image of such an entity appear on TV, instead of a photograph? Ernst replied that the entities themselves have explained this incongruity by the fact that they no longer have physical bodies, so they have no physical images to project. Therefore they make use of images of themselves recorded in photographs while they were still living on Earth. In this manner they seek to identify themselves and offer proof of personality survival after death. Ernst then played a tape of Raudive identifying himself and greeting his listeners in a deep, raspy, eerie voice. People who have heard the tape, and who knew Raudive well, are certain that it is his voice.

§

By this time it was quite late, and I was struggling with a bad case of jet lag, so we made arrangements to meet later when we would travel to the Moselle valley to meet Adolf Homes, one of the most successful experimenters of ITC at present. Two days later we were on our way to Rivenich, where Adolf Homes has a successful antique-repairing business. The drive lasted about an hour, and as we came out of the car, happy to stretch our legs, the door of the cottage opened and out stepped Adolf Homes.

If Ernst Senkowski may be described as a small, amiable elf, Adolf Homes may be described as an equally amiable giant. Easily towering over us, at least 6'6" above the ground, he greeted us warmly and invited us into the house. There we happily finished several bottles of ice wine as Homes explained his involvement with ITC.

Homes lost his mother when he was a small boy. As he had no immediate family, he was placed in an orphanage, where he grew up very lonely, always yearning for his mother's love. After he left the orphanage and began his apprenticeship repairing antiques, he heard a radio transmission from Luxembourg where Ernst Senkowski was talking about voices of the dead captured on tape, especially those of Raudive and Jurgenson. The program made a deep impression on Homes, but it wasn't until several years later that he plucked up enough courage to try transcommunication on his own. At the time there was an organization in Germany whose members were studying voices on tape, and they gave Homes instructions on how to do the ITC experimentation.

He began with one recorder and a quiet room. He could hear vague sounds on the tape, but he was not satisfied. He wanted to make sure that he was receiving actual transmissions from the other side and not simply imagining them. Then the voices became clearer. One night in a dream he got the idea to use five radios simultaneously. After this he could make out distinct messages in German, although he was using shortwave radios with many languages mixed in. One message said: "You close your eyes, the wind blows away, and your heart is broken." At first Homes thought he was going to die, but then it was explained to him that this was simply a metaphor describing the moment of physical death.

All this time Homes thought constantly about his mother and in his mind asked her to communicate with him. "Where are you?" he would ask her. "Are you really dead forever? Is it true that people sleep after death and rise on the last day?" He questioned her continuously and received no answer. This went on for years. Then, one day, she was there. This happened in 1988. Her voice was not found on any tape but came directly through the loudspeakers, an instantaneous transmission. She said: "This is your mother. We are greeting you. All friends are greeting you. You have found the boat." This last metaphor was taken to mean that Homes had found the means to go across to the other side. This initial contact with his mother increased with time. Eventually she became the main communicator between Homes and other entities.

During this period, Homes met Ernst Senkowski, and they began collaborating on many ITC experiments. Homes moved from radio to TV and then to computers. He developed great sensitivity and was able to establish many communications with outside entities through several media. The gist of the information received through him from disembodied beings, corroborated by other ITC experimenters, including Ernst, is as follows:

> *The spirit or mind continues to live after physical death. In some ways the world into which the spirit or disembodied personality finds itself is very similar to the material world, but it is a world where reality may be altered at will. A spirit can reshape its surroundings and its perceptions as if they were made of plaster.*

There are different levels of being in this world, which is described as many worlds in one.

When a spirit is reborn, it comes into the type of surrounding it has prepared for itself in its previous life. The spirit, upon the death of the body, passes on to the other side with its own consciousness, and there seems to be another kind of logic in this other world. Once the spirit adapts to this new logic, it finds it very strenuous to return to our type of logic. From this we can surmise that they are experiencing another type of consciousness, which depends on another perception of time quite different from our own.

People who pass over into this other world are then considered to be multidimensional beings with multidimensional personalities. Under this concept, when a spirit is born anew, it may be born into more than one body simultaneously. This is possible because every human spirit has multiple dimensions and a multiple consciousness. Also, the spirit experiences all his or her lives or incarnations as a whole, simultaneously, not just one life at a time. During a transcommunication with a living human being, a spirit uses names and images to make us understand that it has survived physical death. But neither names nor images have any meaning in the other side.

These messages have been coming through since 1986. At first people thought they were part of a complex hoax, but then it turned out that many of the messages received by Homes had also been received by a team of researchers from Luxembourg at the same time, but independently of each other. In other words, most of the latter transcommunications came through Homes's Commodore 64 at the exact time they were being received by the Luxembourg team.

That same morning, before we had started our drive from Mainz to Rivenich, Homes called Ernst to tell him he had received a message through the computer that he wanted me to see. This message came from a former colleague, now deceased, who simply wanted to reiterate the importance of the power of love in the universe and the eternal bonds of affection that link the living and the dead long after death has separated them. But although Homes sat for some time at his computer while I was there, and asked for a transmission, no one answered his call. I was therefore unable to see an actual transcommunication take place and cannot report on how such messages come through the computer.

Later on, Ernst expressed his belief that the best receivers of transcommunications are psychically gifted people. But he warns that any attempt to contact the dead or alien entities, known scientifically as dynamic informational structures, is potentially dangerous to the psyche. He believes that it is possible to open involuntarily what he calls the PSI barrier, which represents a natural protection against a spiritual or mental "overload." Should this happen, all sorts of phantasmagorical apparitions or voices may appear to the experimenter, which may lead to possession or mental imbalance. Other experimenters share this concern and warn against what they call "mediumistic psychosis," where a person's obsession with the dead may result in acute schizophrenia.

Interpretations of messages from outside entities should therefore be carried out carefully and systematically. The audible voices (sometimes similar to the person's voice during his or her lifetime) as well as the TV projections (similar to the disembodied entity while he or she was alive) should be considered projections from the other world adapted to our sense of reality. The "real" structures or images and voices as experienced in different states of consciousness cannot be transposed into our human awareness. Thus, ITC consists primarily of a more or less unconscious telepathic connection between the entity and the experimenter, whose psychokinetic faculties are activated to inject the message into one of the technical devices used. This hypothesis does not exclude the possibility that these devices are being consciously manipulated by entities outside our world.

In Ernst Senkowski's words, "We are living in a world of probabilities in which practically everything is possible." With the help of our motivations and emotions—our minds—we are able to influence the possibilities and turn them into probabilities. Everybody and everything in this holistic system is interconnected; there are only differences in the strength of conscious awareness. In the mind region there exists no space and no time. Life under these conditions consists of information exchanges or communications according to higher resonance principles. Evolution—fighting entropy—leads to ever more complex systems by trial and error, by learning and adapting.

I had many other questions to ask Homes, but I had to be at the airport in less than two hours, and we still had to drive from Rivenich to Frankfurt. We left Rivenich an hour and a half before my flight time. I had great doubts I would get to the airport in time, and I wondered if I could make another connection to New York. I need not have worried. Adelhaide zoomed through the traffic at demonic speeds and delivered me to the gates of Lufthansa with a few minutes to spare. We all hugged and said our goodbyes, but I knew I had made new friends that would be for a lifetime— or maybe longer, if ITC claims prove to be true.

§

after death

what happens

searching for the soul in princeton

what happens

after death

3 THE IDEA THAT WE MAY BE ABLE to communicate with the disembodied spirit or consciousness of a deceased person through an electronic device such as a radio, a television, or a computer seems so bizarre that many people simply shake their heads and dismiss the concept as total nonsense. But the idea is not as far-fetched as it may sound. This interaction between human consciousness and machines is now being tested with impressive results in a Princeton laboratory.

The experiment, which is being conducted under the strictest protocol, is at the core of the Princeton Engineering Anomalies Research (PEAR) program. The PEAR program is headed by Robert G. Jahn, a professor of aerospace sciences and dean emeritus of the School of Engineering and Applied Science at Princeton University, and Brenda J. Dunne, manager of the PEAR laboratory.

Since PEAR's inception in 1979, Professor Jahn and Ms. Dunne have written over a dozen scholarly papers about the program, its central premise, and the results they have accumulated in over fifteen years of continued studies. More recently, in an attempt to make their findings more accessible to a broader audience, they have published a book entitled *Margins of Reality, The Role of Consciousness in the Physical World*. The book goes into greater detail about the objectives of PEAR and what they have discovered so far.

Although the PEAR program was established in the spring of 1979, its foundation was laid two years earlier when an undergraduate student, an electrical engineering and computer science major, asked Professor Jahn to supervise the design and implementation of an electronic device he wished to use to study low-level psychokinetic effects. Psychokinesis (PK) may be defined as the hypothetical influence of mind over animate or inanimate matter without the use of any known physical or sensory means. It includes such paranormal phenomena as telekinesis (the ability to move objects with the mind), levitation, materialization, paranormal healing, and other "supernatural" effects. Most psychokinetic phenomena are studied through parapsychology and as a rule are not taken seriously by academic communities. It was therefore with the greatest trepidation that Professor Jahn agreed to supervise the project. Years later he would concede that the idea of an experiment concerning psychokinesis created a deep conflict between what he called his personal intellectual skepticism and the potential pedagogical benefits of such a project.

When the student graduated, Professor Jahn was still unconvinced of the viability of the project. However, his curiosity led him to undertake the organization, funding, and supervision of a more substantial research program directly addressing "man/machine anomalies," which are strange and unexplainable phenomena surrounding the interaction between a machine and a human mind. This is how the PEAR program came into being.

The PEAR program, which is completely funded through private funds, is centered around three different types of studies of paranormal phenomena. The first deals with a group of experiments investigating the interactions of human consciousness with various electronic devices, systems, and processes. The results of these experiments have yielded significant deviations from those expected according to established scientific premises. The second study concerns the phenomenon of precognition by which an operator is able to reveal information about a distant location inaccessible by any known communication channel. The third study deals with the development of a theoretical model that may be used to correlate the first two types of experiments, to design other, more in-depth tests, and last, to find explanations for all the various phenomena studied. Because paranormal phenomena such as psychokinesis and precognition are subjects that most scientists cringe away from, it is important that the PEAR experiments be conducted under the most rigorous scientific control. PEAR's objective is the scientific validation of psychokinesis and precognition; for that reason, all the experiments are carefully designed so that they may be easily replicable. Replication, when an experiment is reproduced in a laboratory under the exact conditions as the original experiment, is vital if a scientific project is to be seriously considered by the scientific community.

The one aspect of the PEAR research that interests us here is the first of their three fields of study, which deals with psychokinesis, or the interaction between human consciousness and electronic devices or machines. The particular experiments conducted at the PEAR lab on psychokinesis involve an operator—an unpaid volunteer of either sex who is not specially gifted psychically—and a machine known as a Random Event Generator (REG). This machine is based on a source of white noise that is generated electronically. The circuitry of the machine transforms the noise into a regularly spaced series of alternating binary (negative or positive) pulses, very similar to the flipping of a coin, where heads may be represented by a positive pulse and tails by a negative pulse. The operator, who sits in front of the machine, attempts to influence the pulses, willing a specific outcome, such as a majority of positive pulses. Scientifically, the distribution of results may be compared with Gaussian prediction, which is a theoretical frequency distribution for a set of variable data. Through this, it would be possible to calculate statistically the likelihood that the achieved distribution could have occurred by chance versus the possibility that it could have happened through the applied volition (or mental power) of the operator trying to influence the Random Event Generator.

PEAR results indicate that the operator's will is able to influence the REG system. The effects that are being produced might be considered small in another system. They are, in fact, in the order of a few bits (units of information storage capacity) per 10,000 tries. But in an informational system such as REG, which deals in tens of millions of bits, an alteration of a few bits on the law of averages can have a substantial implication.

After my return from Mainz, I spoke with Brenda Dunne, who is the laboratory manager as well as Robert Jahn's main collaborator in the PEAR experiments. She acceded to an interview during which she could show me the lab and explain at some length the way the experiments are conducted and their general views on the survival of the personality or human consciousness after the death of the physical body.

I had visited Princeton two years earlier when I took part in a symposium on religion, and I was glad to be back on the beautiful and serene campus once more. When Brenda took me to the lab where the experiments are being conducted, I was very surprised to find a completely different environment than I had anticipated. Instead of white walls, sterile cubicles, and people in white coats, I found a very relaxed and cozy atmosphere, very much like someone's favorite den. There were stuffed animals everywhere, and large, comfortable sofas. The room where the experiments are conducted is also pleasant and informal. The formidable Random Event Generator turned out to be a medium-sized metal box of a very unassuming appearance. Other "props" used in the experiments, such as a large, beautiful drum rigged electronically to produce evenly spaced drumming sounds, were casually placed around the room. Brenda explained that the relaxed environment is important to the experiments because the operators are encouraged to be as comfortable as possible during their trials with the REG. The harder a person tries to influence the machine, the lesser are his or her chances to succeed. It is only when the person is totally at ease and relaxed that the best results are obtained.

I then asked Brenda to explain in some detail the work done at the lab and how it may relate to the survival of the human personality or consciousness after we die. One could argue, she said, that the most elaborate and amazing information-processing device system is the human mind. What the mind, the consciousness, does best is to organize information. We take information from the environment, process it, categorize it, identify it, and classify it. We then project it back into the environment. When we encounter a new event, we don't have any idea of what it may be, but after we process it and identify it, we will be able to recognize it the next time we encounter it. With each new encounter, we add more data to the files we have stored on that event, we assign some probability, and then we are able to interact more effectively with the world as a result of the information we have acquired through the processes of the consciousness. The experiments done at the PEAR lab, both the operator/REG test and the remote-perception test, have told the PEAR staff that these information processes appear to be independent of the strain of time and space. People involved in the remote-perception experiment are able to acquire information from paranormal sources about locations that not only are thousands of miles away but have not been revealed to them. Also, people who are involved in the operator/REG experiment seem to be able to affect the outcome of the output by thinking about the machine when it is not even running. These experiments suggest that contrary to traditional thought, the human mind is not constrained or totally dependent on the physical body.

At this point I asked Brenda if she believed that the mind or human consciousness exists independently of the brain. This is a controversial concept that has often set academicians at war with each other, and I wanted to know PEAR's position on the subject. She candidly agreed that the mind acts independently of the brain and added that the experiments at PEAR seem to indicate that the mind or consciousness is a not a tangible, physical object like the brain. Rather, the mind is a process, a principle of organization, that enables the individual to interact with his or her environment. The brain acts as a receiver, a processor, very much like a computer. The consciousness organizes the information it gathers from the environment, which the brain then translates into thoughts, ideas, and concepts.

The model that PEAR proposes as a result of their experiments uses quantum mechanics as a metaphor. The model says in fact that everything that exists is a construction of consciousness, whether we are referring to consciousness, the physical body, an abstract concept, or a religious dogma—any model of reality. In other words, reality is created by the mind itself. It is an expression of how the consciousness/mind organizes the information it gathers from the environment to create a definite structure that is identifiable. If one accepts this premise, then one can look at any model of reality, anything that exists, and realize that these models are giving us information not only about the physical world but also about how we experience and express the physical world, and how consciousness organizes information.

What PEAR did was look at quantum mechanics in a metaphorical sense to see what it told them about how consciousness generates reality. What came out of this metaphor has some bearing on the human personality. In physics there is a wave/particle duality: sometimes physics perceives the physical world in terms of a wave and other times in terms of particles. The PEAR researchers then asked themselves the following question: If consciousness has decided to assign this wave/particle complement to the physical world, why not assign it to ourselves as well? We usually think of ourselves as particles, each of us centered in our brains, interacting with each other in a collisional fashion. Waves, on the other hand, can do things particles cannot. Waves can diffract and, most importantly, can resonate, establishing resonance when two of them face each other.

One of the ways in which waves relate to the physical world is the fact that they have environmental potential. A wave function has no definable characteristics except perhaps a frequency and an amplitude, but it can be anywhere at any time. If you place a wave in a given environment, like a box, it sets standing-wave patterns. The wave is now localized in space and time. These standing-wave patterns, which physicists call eigenfunctions, are essentially information about that particular wave function in that particular environment. The human consciousness is probably a type of wave function, which some people would call soul or spirit. When that wave function is not localized in time and space—that is, it is not confined to a physical body or environment—it may or may not have a definite personality. But when it interacts in a given environment, such as the physical body, designed or determined by a DNA structure and other material factors, those same environmental factors condition that wave function and produce a personality. Conversely, if you take away those environmental constraints, you still have a wave function that will retain or reflect a certain amount of the information obtained from its environment, but because it is no longer constrained by the environment, many of its former characteristics would tend to disappear. This is what probably happens at the moment of physical death. There would be something left, but not the same type of wave function that existed within the confines of the environment because now that wave function is free from its former environment. If you put that wave function into a different environment, it would have different characteristics, which raises some interesting questions concerning the possibility of reincarnation.

I then asked how such a wave function would become localized as a human being. Brenda explained that the wave exists in all time and space, but that it is unclear how it becomes "caught" in the environment. It could be chance, or it may choose to interact with the environment and become part of the physical world. When I asked how long this wave would survive, Brenda explained that according to the laws of physics, a wave exists in all space and in all time. In other words, it is infinite.

The conversation then turned philosophical, and we discussed the effects of meditation and the possibilities of other dimensions or levels of being. This raised the question that after we die, the consciousness/mind, now disembodied, may have experiences and knowledge to impart, but how these experiences could be described or communicated becomes a separate conundrum.

It is undeniable that the work being done by PEAR is not only groundbreaking but of great importance in understanding the paranormal abilities of the human mind. In view of the position that science has traditionally adopted on all extrasensory phenomena, the members of the PEAR program, all of them reputable scientists, have shown unusual courage pursuing their conviction of the existence of extrasensory powers in the human mind and of a spiritual reality that extends beyond the realms of the space-time continuum.

After we finished the interview, Brenda made an interesting comment on the now classical division between science and mysticism. She said that some people are torn between their rational minds and their spiritual yearnings. They feel compelled to choose one over the other, being unable to accept both. So either they choose science at the cost of their souls, or they choose the spiritual path and lose their capacity to rationalize. We shouldn't have to choose, she added. Science and religion are forever intertwined. We have officially disengaged our science from our spirituality; this is an artificial decision. If we don't find a way to reintegrate them, we are going to be faced with disaster.

§

after death

what happens

the astral world

what happens

after death

4 THE WORD *ASTRAL* IS DERIVED from the Greek word *astron,* which means "of the stars." The word was originally used to refer to the abode of the Greek gods, but its meaning later grew to include other entities and other planes. The ancients believed that "the astral world" was a phantasmagorical place populated by ethereal beings and angels belonging to the higher hierarchies. Eventually, the term "astral world" or "astral plane" became identified with the occult sciences, and currently it is considered a mysterious, spatial zone that is said to exist beyond our normal senses and our material perceptions.

Several years ago I read a small treatise entitled *The Astral World,* written by a Hindu master called Swami Panchadasi. The book caught my attention because its author presented his case with great insight, making good use of his considerable knowledge of the physical sciences, as well as biochemistry, history, literature, and philosophy. The subject he wrote about is not an easy one to discuss as it tends to stretch the imagination beyond all reasonable boundaries. But he wrote so convincingly, with such natural candor, that he nearly forced his reader to believe his presentation, some of which verged on the surreal. Because of the clarity of his exposition and because it is also the traditional explanation that the various mystery schools give us of the astral world, I have chosen to use Panchadasi's presentation of the theme here.

The ancient teachings tell us there are seven planes of existence. The first plane, and the densest of the seven, is the material plane, which is identified with our physical world. The second is the force plane, also known as the etheric plane. This is followed by the third, or astral, plane, and this by the fourth, or mental, plane. The three planes that follow the first four are said to be of such a high degree of spiritual evolution that very little is known about them.

Each of these seven planes is divided into seven sub-planes, each of which in turn is divided into seven subdivisions, which continue to be likewise divided until they have reached the seventh degree of subdivision. Panchadasi tells us that these planes are not superimposed upon each other as they would be if they were part of the Earth's strata; rather, they are all manifest in the same point in space. To understand their essence, it is important to remember that with the exception of the material plane, they have no physical substance. They are manifestations of energy in varying degrees of vibration. The densest and slowest of these vibrations produces the material plane, or physical world. The higher and faster vibrations produce other planes, other worlds, among which is the astral world.

If the planes are conceived as energy manifestations of increasing vibratory rates, then it is also possible to conceive that they may all be located on the same point in space, but at different densities, each one subtler than the last. The best way to understand this concept is by remembering that heat, electricity, magnetism, x-rays, laser beams, and ultraviolet light can all exist in the same space without interfering with each other because they all consist of energies moving at different vibratory rates. In the same way, different planes can coexist at the same point of physical space without impinging upon each other. Some of the ancient masters tried to explain this idea by saying that a plane is not a place but a state of being.

The second plane, known as the force plane or etheric plane, is where we find the creative energies through which the Universe came into being. In recent years, physicists, especially those studying quantum mechanics, have been studying the energies of the etheric plane without realizing it. It is in this plane that we find subatomic particles such as neutrinos, muons, and quarks, which some physicists believe may be the building blocks of matter. The etheric substance known as prana, one of the forces created in this plane, and which we absorb with each breath, is our true source of sustenance according to the yogis. Prana is best assimilated into the organism through a pattern of rhythmic breathing known as pranayama.

The third plane, known as the astral plane or astral world, is the state of being that is reached by the human spirit after we die. It is also where we sojourn each night during our dreams. The astral plane is accessible to a living human being either by using the astral senses or by traveling to these inner regions with the astral body.

The astral senses are directly connected with the physical senses, and it is through these that humans receive input from the astral world. In other words, each of our five senses—sight, touch, hearing, smell, and taste—has a counterpart in the astral world. There are other senses in the astral plane that we know as extrasensory perception (ESP), among which are telepathy, psychokinesis, and clairvoyance. These senses are dormant in most humans but are slowly awakening. Clairvoyants sometimes have astral visions, but these are usually spontaneous, not controlled. True astral vision is acquired only through special studies and exercises. People who have developed this faculty can use it to transcend from one plane to another through the force of will.

Astral travel, according to Panchadasi, is a method of moving through the various planes using the astral body. This body is formed of an etheric substance that has a very high vibratory rate, and it is where the human personality normally resides. Although it is very tenuous, it is possible to perceive the astral body under certain circumstances. Normally the astral body surrounds the physical body like a translucent sheath, and it may be perceived as a bluish gray halo that extends a few inches beyond the skin. The color may change depending on the health, mental, or moral state of a person. This halo is commonly known as a person's aura and is not difficult to see. An easy way to perceive the aura is by holding an arm horizontally against a light background and then looking just above the skin while letting the eyes go slightly out of focus. Within minutes it is possible to see the aura as a faint, bluish gray band extending the length of the arm.

The astral body is an exact copy of the physical body and survives after the physical body dies. However, the astral body is not immortal and eventually disintegrates and returns to its component parts, as does the physical body. Many people have had out-of-body experiences where they have found themselves floating outside their physical body. Some claim to have traveled to strange regions and, upon returning to their body, have found it cold and inert, like a vacant house. All of these are examples of astral travels where an individual has moved outside the physical realm in the astral body.

People who are clairvoyant or have conscious astral vision tell us that the astral body is connected to the physical body by a cord that resembles a wisp of grayish silver smoke that can connect the two bodies across long distances. This celebrated silver cord breaks at the time of death, allowing the astral body and the spirit to leave the physical body.

At this point it is important to clarify that the astral body is not the spirit or consciousness of an individual but rather what is known as the soul, which is the union of the etheric and the astral bodies. The etheric body is the sum total of the human instincts, while the astral body is the seat of the emotions. The spirit is a combination of mind, logic, reason, inspiration, and all the esoteric qualities of a human being.

The astral body is therefore an amalgam of the instincts and emotions of a person. While this person is alive, all journeys taken in the astral body become part of his or her consciousness, spirit, and personality. When people travel in the astral world they perceive it as if it were the material world. There are cities, landscapes, forests, rivers, fields, people, and many more things in this strange world. Material things appear as real in the context of the astral world as they do in the material world.

It is possible to travel from one place to another in the astral world solely by an act of will. In other words, one may travel to any given place simply by wishing it. Many different types of beings can be found in this unearthly world; among these are the astral bodies of people who have died, as well as entities who have never lived in the material world because they are denizens of the astral. Fairies, gnomes, elves, nyads, salamanders, undines, sirens, devas, genies, and other beings who have long populated our imagination—all are part of the ethereal realm of the astral plane. They exist there because we have conjured them into existence by envisioning them through a myriad of folktales, thus giving each of them a life of its very own. Everything we can imagine is immediately created in the astral world and is as real there as we have imagined it to be, which is the reason thoughts are so powerful and so potentially dangerous if not properly controlled.

§

The first subplane of the astral world, what Panchadasi calls the astral cemetery, is where the astral bodies of people who have died go to await disintegration. When a person dies, the spirit, along with the astral body, goes to one of the subplanes of the astral world, where it rests in a peaceful and regenerative sleep. During this sleep the spirit is prepared for the place that corresponds to its level of spiritual development. When the spirit awakens, it immediately passes to the mental plane, where it then proceeds to the level corresponding to its development. The astral body remains in the astral world for a short time after the spirit leaves it.

Eventually the astral body loses strength and disintegrates like the physical body. When this happens, it immediately passes to the astral cemetery. The more spiritually advanced a person is, the faster his or her astral body will disintegrate, as it is composed mostly of the person's instincts and emotions. The more attached a person is to the physical world, the longer his or her astral body will remain in the lower planes of the astral world.

According to Panchadasi, it is the astral bodies, not the spirits of people who have died, who communicate through séances or channeling sessions. These are also the ghosts who haunt and follow the living, unable to find a resting place. This is particularly true of people who die violently and are unable to reconcile themselves to their deaths.

After we die, the spirit normally regenerates itself in the astral world and then passes directly to the mental plane. But the astral body can retain certain memories and aspects of the personality that make it possible for it to establish a communication, however tenuous, with the living. People at a séance want to be convinced that the entity with whom they are communicating is the spirit of someone they once knew or loved. An observant person, however, will realize that the entity they are contacting is unconvincing and that its actions or apparent behavior is not exactly the same as that of the living entity it claims to have once inhabited. There appears to be something missing in the disembodied entity. Panchadasi says that what is missing is the spark of the spirit, of the mind that has already gone on to higher planes, leaving behind an empty shell, the remnants of the soul.

Panchadasi also says that after death most spirits "sleep" for a long time, some for many years, in the subplanes of the astral world. People who are highly evolved spiritually and people at the bottom of the spiritual ladder both awake after shorter periods, the spiritually elevated because they do not need much time to prepare for their corresponding level in the mental world and the spiritually unevolved because they automatically gravitate to areas of lower vibration. Once in these zones, they continue to relive the same terrible, destructive actions that characterized their material lives, but only as helpless spectators. Eventually, many of these spirits become horrified at the visions of their past lives, repent of their actions, and try to leave these subplanes and ascend to higher levels of being. When this happens, the force of their desire to evolve helps them rise to higher planes, giving them the hope of purification. There are those, however, who have descended so low on the spiritual scale that they are unable or unwilling to reject their past actions. Without this repentance, and the desire to ascend to regions of greater light, the spirit runs the risk of eventual disintegration. These subplanes of the lower astral world have been equated with hell and purgatory.

Unlike its terrifying sublevels, the astral world has higher regions where those spirits who were creative in the physical world, such as writers, painters, poets, and composers, can bring to fruition great works that were left unfinished on the material plane. Others create wonderful works in the astral plane that are later perceived as inspirations by human beings, who carry them through to completion in the physical world.

The astral world is the womb of the physical plane. Everything that takes place in the material world is but an echo of something that has already happened in the astral world, which is also the world of imagination. That is why it is possible to create and visualize things with our minds that later are materialized in the physical world.

In the mental plane, we find the higher regions that many religions call heavens. In these subplanes are found the exalted spirits of highly evolved human beings, such as saints and martyrs, and those who sacrificed their lives for others or in the pursuit of sublime ideals. Angels, whose essence is pure love, belong to the highest regions of the astral plane but travel continually among the higher planes.

Panchadasi, a firm believer in reincarnation, tells us that highly evolved spirits take a much longer time to reincarnate. When such a being elects to be reborn soon after its last existence, it is making a supreme sacrifice, usually for an important reason. When it is born anew, it is deprived of the great joy and ecstasies that are the continuous life of the spirit on the higher planes.

In the astral world there are sub planes that correspond to the "paradises" of the ancient warrior races. Here we find the Valhalla of the Vikings, the Elysian Fields of the ancient Greeks, and the Happy Hunting Grounds of the American Indians.

Almost all spirits, from the most to the least evolved, spend some time in the subplanes of the astral world, where they endeavor to perfect themselves and acquire a higher elevation. Before a spirit can reincarnate, it must leave the astral world and pass to the proper subplane in the mental world. The less-evolved spirits spend little time here and reincarnate quickly, as this allows them to evolve faster. A highly evolved spirit can spend centuries in the regions of the mental world or in some of the higher planes. During its stay in these high dimensions, the spirit enters into a total identification with its Higher Self from which it receives purification and light, thus enjoying the divine ecstasy yogis know as Nirvana. If the spirit is so far evolved that it no longer needs to reincarnate, it stays in the superior planes, where it may help those spirits still bound to the incarnation cycle.

So far we have been discussing the ideas of Swami Panchadasi to explain the astral world. Naturally there is no concrete evidence to prove the existence of this nebulous region, but there are some tantalizing new findings in the fields of physics and astronomy that may shed some light on the subject. Astronomers are now talking of a dark, invisible matter that forms most of the Universe. Nobody knows what it is made of, but it appears to be about ten times more abundant than all of the material contained in the stars. Maybe an understanding of this dark substance can provide us with answers to the important questions we are asking about the cosmos. It may answer our questions about the future of the Universe, its beginning, and its eventual end. We may even wonder if the mysterious astral world is in fact a part of this invisible Universe.

§

after death

what happens

**the
tunnel**

what happens

after death

5 **ONE OF THE MOST COMMON** experiences related by those who have been revived after a clinical death involves the now-famous tunnel of light. People say that while they were in this apparent death state, they were propelled through a tunnel of light at the end of which they encountered a Christlike figure or figure of light. In most cases this ethereal figure compelled them to return to their earthly bodies, something they seemed reluctant to do. Similar experiences have been related by people close to death.

The tunnel of light is not the only experience reported by people who have been clinically dead or on the brink of death. There are also stories of those who have encountered deceased friends or members of their families. One of these stories made its way to a major New York television channel in the late seventies. The story concerned a twenty-year-old man who was brutally stabbed in the streets of Lower Manhattan and nearly drained of blood by the time he was found and brought to the emergency room of Bellevue Hospital. The doctors in the ER could not detect any vital signs and pronounced him dead on arrival. But, seeing how young the man was, one of the resident physicians decided to try to revive him. The young man was taken to an operating room, where the physician proceeded to close the wounds. Transfusions were given to try to reactivate a heart that had stopped beating due to lack of blood.

While the doctor battled to save the young man's life, his patient had a vision where he saw himself looking down on these efforts while he floated near the ceiling of the operating theater. Afterward, he described how he watched the frenetic activity below with a sense of great calm, wondering why so much effort was being wasted on saving his life when he was perfectly content as he was. Then the ceiling suddenly opened to reveal several beings closely watching the work being performed on the inert body below. Among these faces, the young man recognized his older brother, who had been killed in a car accident several years earlier. He felt a strong desire to join his brother and tried to pass through the gap in the ceiling to be with him. But his brother pushed him back, saying, "You can't come in. There is no space for you here. You have to go back." The young man begged his brother to let him in, but was met with repeated refusals. The brother then violently pushed him away, so that the young man landed back in his body lying on the operating table. Immediately the head surgeon cried out, "We have a pulse!" as doctors and nurses intensified their efforts to sustain the life that had miraculously returned. The young man was still in a wheelchair when he went before the television cameras several weeks later, tearfully recounting his experience and still claiming that he would have preferred to join his brother in that unearthly realm rather than return to the physical world.

Recently the young husband of one of my students told me a similar story. This young man, whom we will call Paul, went with some friends to a bachelor party in honor of a mutual friend. Shortly after midnight, one of the men present at the party, who had been jilted by the bride-to-be, pulled out a gun and started firing into the crowd. Fortunately no one was killed, but a bullet entered Paul's neck at the base of the throat and lodged itself within inches of his left lung. Paul collapsed in a fountain of blood and was immediately rushed to a nearby hospital, where doctors began a desperate effort to save his life.

While all this commotion was going on around him, Paul felt himself slipping out of his body through his feet, very much like a thin handkerchief that blows away in the wind. He then found himself in a long queue where many people were waiting in line to be judged. One of the people in line was an old friend of Paul's who had died several weeks earlier in a car accident. The two friends spoke very naturally, and as they spoke, Paul heard a beautiful melody that he had never heard before. There were many strange flowers around the place in colors he could not describe, as they do not exist on Earth. Those present, himself included, were dressed in long gowns in soft pastel colors.

Suddenly, the imposing figure of an elderly man dressed in shimmering white appeared on the scene. He looked serenely around, and immediately noticed Paul and a little girl who was behind him. "You two," he called out in a thundering voice. "What are you doing here?" Paul answered for himself and for the little girl. "We are waiting to be judged." The old man shook his head. "You have nothing to do here. You have to go back, both of you, right now. It's not your time yet." With that, he made a dismissive gesture with his hand. At that precise moment, Paul felt as if he had fallen back into his body from a great height, and he heard a doctor's voice say to his sobbing wife, "It's all right, he's going to make it." As he told this story, he wondered if the little girl who had been with him had also made it back.

There are many stories like these. One of the most famous books on the near-death experience is undoubtedly *Life after Life*, written by Dr. Raymond A. Moody. The book summarizes Dr. Moody's studies of hundreds of cases of people who have returned to life after being pronounced clinically dead.

The notable exceptions in the case histories collected by Dr. Moody were people whose near-death experiences had been caused by suicide attempts. These people recounted terrifying experiences that caused them to repent and return to change their lives. All of these people said that their near-death experiences left them with the impression that "suicide is not a way out since the personality continues to live" and that "in the other life the suicidal person is punished for his or her actions."

One of the more interesting experiences Dr. Moody encountered was that of a woman who told of an elderly aunt who was seriously ill. The whole family was praying for the old woman's recovery. The aunt had stopped breathing several times, but each time doctors were able to revive her. Finally, the aunt called her niece to her bedside and said that she had visited the "other world" where people went when they died. It was a beautiful place, and she wanted to stay there, but the family's prayers were keeping her alive. She asked to be allowed to die in peace. The niece conveyed the request to the other members of the family, and prayers for the old woman's recovery were duly suspended. She died shortly afterward.

§

Dr. Moody is not the only scientist investigating life after death. Another researcher, Dr. Elizabeth Kubler-Ross, has also done many detailed studies on the subject. Several years ago, researchers from the medical school at the University of Connecticut also began a study of near-death experiences. What these scientists find fascinating is the fact that so many people who have been pronounced clinically dead report traveling through a dark tunnel to a source of light for encounters with a Christlike figure or with departed loved ones. Naturally, only Christians see the Christ figure. People of other religions see angels or sacred figures related to their own beliefs.

Several years ago, while I was still living in Vienna and working for the United Nations, I had an out-of-body experience. It was a time of great personal peace and harmony. I was lying in bed but not yet asleep when I heard the rattling sound described by some of Dr. Moody's subjects. At the same instant, I felt myself rising out of my body at an astonishing speed until I was suddenly floating near the ceiling. I had the initial impression that I was growing very fast, but I was simply rushing toward the ceiling. The most remarkable part of the experience was that at no time did I feel that what was happening was strange or frightening. On the contrary, I accepted this extraordinary situation very calmly. As I floated near the ceiling the rattling sound was intensified, and suddenly I felt a powerful force pulling me toward one corner of the ceiling. My thought at that moment was, "My God, I'm going to die." I only had time to say, "My God, in your hands I entrust my soul" before I was rushed at an indescribable speed through a perfectly dark vacuum and I lost all consciousness. I don't know where I went while I was "outside" my body or indeed if I went anywhere. The next thing I remember is floating near the ceiling once again and feeling a great desire to return to my body. No sooner did I wish it than I was back in my body. I still remember how still and cold it felt, like a house that has been empty for a long time.

These experiences lend strength to the belief that the strange phenomenon we call the mind is not directly associated with the body in general or the brain in particular. The mind can exist independently of the body. As we saw from the PEAR experiments, there is enough scientific evidence at present to support this theory.

It is tempting to think that people who have left their body during a grave illness or clinical death, or those like me who were not ill but left their body momentarily, are proof of life after death. But we must remember that none of these people actually died. All they had was an out-of-body experience. All the people who have reported visions of the "other world"—like the woman who asked her niece not to pray for her—were alive when they had the experience. Unfortunately, no one yet has returned several years after death to tell us about his or her experience, except through séances or channeling sessions, which in themselves cannot be accepted as proofs of survival.

This means one of two things. Either the experience of leaving the body is a brief hallucination caused by a spontaneous malfunction of the organism, specifically the brain, or it is the result of a brief separation of the spirit from the material body, as explained by the yogis. The experience may be induced by trauma while the person is on the brink of death, by fatigue, or by intense mystical or meditation practices.

Some biochemists believe that the vision of an afterlife or out-of-body experiences are caused by a hallucinogenic substance created by the pineal gland. According to these scientists, this chemical is produced at the onset of death or danger of death to soften the terrible trauma the human brain experiences at the end of life. In this way it makes the death transition easier, less frightening, and more acceptable to the dying person. This theory may offer an explanation of why a dying person has these visions, but it does not explain the out-of-body experiences of those who are not sick or near death.

Maybe the projection of the astral body is an experience that happens only to the living. Maybe death is the end of everything. But then again, maybe it is not. Maybe the experience of astral projection, the tunnel of light, the luminous figures, the beautiful regions of the astral plane, and the visions of dead relatives and friends are proof that the personality survives the experience of death.

One of the more fascinating recent discoveries is the existence of so-called black holes. Astronomers tell us that these cosmic phenomena are created when a star, like our sun, explodes. These exploding stars are known as supernovas. As they develop, the great density of their cores causes them to collapse in upon themselves, creating what scientists call a black hole. The black hole has enormous gravitational pull, drawing everything toward its mysterious interior. One of the many theories about these strange phenomena tells us that they may be gateways to other worlds. The description of the dark tunnel, the intense light, and the Christlike figure is strangely similar to the description of the black hole and its enormous gravitational force. This makes one wonder if the black hole of astrophysics is the gateway to the astral world.

§

after death

what happens

reincarnation

what happens

after death

6 **THE DOCTRINE OF REINCARNA-**
tion can be found in many of the ancient religions and continues to exist in modern times. The Egyptians, Greeks, and Romans all believed in reincarnation. Although Christianity and Judaism both believe in the immortality of the spirit, they do not believe in reincarnation. In both these religions, the principal belief is that after death the spirit goes to either heaven or hell depending on its actions while it was on Earth. Christians also believe the soul is purged of all its earthly sins so that it will be worthy of entering heaven. Christianity teaches us that after the soul leaves the earthly body, it "sleeps" for a long time and is not revived until the day of final judgment, when the Archangel Gabriel blows his trumpet to initiate this apocalyptic awakening.

The theory of reincarnation in modern times is based on the teachings of Hinduism and Buddhism, which teach that the spirit is tied to the wheel of life. The spirit cannot be released from this wheel until it reaches the final stage of development, called Nirvana. At this point the spirit becomes an independent entity and a part of God. According to the Hindus, each incarnation is an opportunity for the individual soul to further purify itself in preparation for the ecstasies of Nirvana. For this to occur, a person must do special exercises and follow a special system of meditation. A vegetarian diet is needed to assist individuals in extricating themselves from the material cycle, with its temptations and false images, until they are able to relinquish the physical world. One of the systems recommended by Hinduism is yoga, especially Hatha Yoga, which specializes in body exercises (asanas), breathing exercises (pranayamas), and a strict vegetarianism, where not only meats but all animal products, including milk and eggs, are avoided.

A typical example of the beliefs of Buddhism is the reincarnation of the Dalai Lama, the spiritual guide of Tibetan Buddhists, who believe that when the Dalai Lama dies, his spirit is immediately reincarnated in the body of a male child born at that exact moment. This child also needs to have the mark of the tiger on his legs, as well as other characteristics specific to the Dalai Lama. When the child is older, he is shown various objects and asked to choose those that belonged to the Dalai Lama. If the boy chooses the correct objects, he is considered to be the reincarnation of the Tibetan master.

§

Many of the Buddhist ideas about reincarnation were adapted into a mystical movement called Theosophy. This was started in New York in 1875 by a Russian immigrant of a somewhat notorious reputation called Madame Helena Petrovna Blavatsky, who had both a great flair for the dramatic and a brilliant intellect. Madame Blavatsky left Russia at an early age and spent the rest of her life traveling around the world, especially Asia, where she claimed to have met spiritual masters who taught her the mysteries of the Universe and chose her to spread these teachings throughout the world. The core of these teachings, which included her theories about reincarnation, were fully expounded in the tenets of the Theosophical Society, which she founded in collaboration with W. Q. Judge and H. S. Olcott. The term "theosophy" is derived from the Greek *theos* (God) and *sophia* (wisdom), and means literally "wisdom of or about God." The two best-known adherents of the Theosophical Society were Annie Besant and Rudolf Steiner. Madame Blavatsky wrote many lengthy treatises of great spiritual depth and uncanny wisdom, among which are *The Secret Doctrine* and *Isis Unveiled.* Her writings have awakened renewed interest in the concept of reincarnation and gained new supporters during the last fifty years.

The doctrine of Theosophy is based on three fundamental propositions. The first presents the concept of an unbounded, eternal, omniscient principle of infinite potentiality that may be identified as the Creative Force of the Universe. The second postulates the universality of natural cycles and the law of periodicity. As morning, noon, and night are succeeded by a new cycle that starts with another morning, so are birth, youth, adulthood, and death succeeded by a new cycle of rebirth with another life, a new incarnation. This concept of reincarnation is seen by Theosophy as a natural process of human evolution in which all changes and development are ruled by the law of karma, or divine justice. The third proposition maintains that all souls are intrinsically bound to the Universal Oversoul with which they are identified. This suggests that kinship is a fact of nature and that every soul must advance and grow through numerous cycles of incarnation. Special gifts and powers can only be attained by human beings through their own efforts toward spiritual development. Perfected individuals and great teachers, such as Buddha and Jesus, are perfectly evolved universal beings.

Unlike the teachings of Hinduism and Buddhism, which tell us that reincarnation is like a wheel to which we are tied, depriving us of union with God, Theosophy says that reincarnation is an evolutionary process through which the spirit advances on the road toward God. The Theosophical doctrine of reincarnation is the one closest to Western spiritualist ideas of life after death.

Many famous historical figures were firm believers in reincarnation, among them Queen Victoria, Benjamin Franklin, General George Patton, and Abraham Lincoln. While there are no conclusive proofs of the veracity of reincarnation, there are many unexplainable phenomena concerning cases of apparent rebirth to make us ponder the very real probabilities of its existence.

৯

One of the most famous proponents of the theory of reincarnation in the United States was the psychic Edgar Cayce. Dozens of books have been written about Cayce, who was better known as "the Sleeping Prophet" because he made most of his prophecies under a light trance. Much of Cayce's work has been compiled in his readings, a collection of prophecies, diagnoses, and cures, all of which came to him while he was in this trancelike state.

There are more than 2,500 prophecies of Cayce's, yet curiously enough, none of his major predictions have come true. For example, 1968 came and went with no sign of the three major events Cayce had predicted for that year—the reappearance of the lost continent of Atlantis off the coast of Bermuda, China's conversion to Christianity, and a massive earthquake that would destroy California. In spite of the failure of these prophecies to materialize, Cayce's beliefs and teachings continue to draw attention, and he still has thousands of followers.

Perhaps the reason why Cayce's readings remain so popular, in spite of the failure of his prophecies, is that they are so easy to accept. Cayce was what we might call a transcendental Christian; that is, his teachings were grounded in those of Jesus but mixed with the theological concepts of Madame Blavatsky and Hindu beliefs such as the concept of karma. For Cayce, karma is not the result of the evil actions of a person, what he called the "entity," during each incarnation or life. According to him, each action—whether good or bad—creates a kind of cosmic echo or boomerang that returns to the individual in one form or another during the next incarnation. This explains all the joys and sufferings a person may experience during his or her lifetime. They are simply the results of previous actions in an earlier incarnation. In other words, they are karmic events.

In spite of his strongly orthodox Christian beliefs, Cayce was a fervent exponent of the theory of reincarnation, which is not part of the teachings of Christianity. He claimed, for example, that during previous incarnations he had been an Arab prince and an Egyptian high priest called Ra-Ta. His wife Gertrudis had also been his wife during his Egyptian incarnation, at which time she had been an exotic dancer in the temple of one of the gods. It is not easy to imagine Gertrudis, a respectable lady of ample proportions, performing the dance of the seven veils, but Cayce maintained that each incarnation was totally different from the previous one. Thus the transformation of the sensuous Egyptian dancer into the generously built Gertrudis fits very well within Cayce's hypothetical concept of the reincarnation phenomenon.

§

One of the most famous examples of reincarnation claims is that of Bridey Murphy, the nineteenth-century Irishwoman who was allegedly reincarnated as an American housewife. The case was told in detail in the book *The Search for Bridey Murphy*, written by Colorado businessman Morey Bernstein. The book was an overnight sensation, selling millions of copies within a few months of its publication and topping bestseller lists all over the world. Bernstein had practiced hypnotism for many years and was a great admirer of Edgar Cayce and a fervent believer in reincarnation.

Bernstein had heard of a hypnotism technique called regression therapy, which was used by psychiatrists to bring patients back to their childhood. Once in a deep hypnotic trance, a patient could be regressed to infancy, allowing the recollection of traumatic events that could help the patient resolve pathological personality disorders. Bernstein had also heard it was possible to use regression therapy to take the subject back into past lives.

Hoping to prove that this was possible, Bernstein began to experiment with a Colorado friend called Virginia Tighe. Their first session took place in November 1952. In a deep hypnotic trance, Virginia began to speak with a strong Irish accent and said she was an eight-year-old girl called Bridey Murphy who had lived with her family in County Cork in 1805. In six subsequent sessions, Bridey—through the hypnotized Virginia—gave extraordinary details of her family, the place where they lived, the stores where they shopped, and many other details of everyday life. A journalist called Barker heard about the case, and his series of articles in a Denver magazine became the basis for Bernstein's book. Suddenly, all America was talking about Bridey Murphy and about reincarnation. It seemed everyone had heard of a similar case or had had a similar experience. The theory of reincarnation had never received better publicity.

Then, almost as suddenly as it had started, this wave of profitable free publicity turned into a torrent of vitriolic attacks against Bridey, Virginia, and Bernstein. The first assault came from psychiatrists enraged by Bernstein's use, or abuse, of regression therapy. They were quickly joined by outraged historians who pointed out many serious mistakes in Bridey's accounts of life in nineteenth-century Ireland. But perhaps the most damning condemnations against Bridey Murphy came from the ranks of the clergy, who claimed the concept of reincarnation contradicted biblical scriptures. They called the theory of rebirth anti-Christian and declared it a potential danger to the teachings of Christianity. All of these various groups began a series of in-depth studies on the claims of Bridey Murphy and Virginia Tighe with the intention of discrediting Bernstein's book. Eventually many errors were found in Bridey's statements, and people began to lose interest in her story. The movie based on the book went virtually unnoticed. Today, the strange story of Bridey Murphy is still viewed with a mixture of doubt and curiosity, and it is unlikely we will ever know if her existence was rooted in historical truth or in the vivid imagination of Virginia Tighe.

§

One of the most interesting books ever written about reincarnation is *Twenty Cases Suggestive of Reincarnation* by Canadian psychiatrist Ian Stevenson. As the title suggests, the book is a compilation of twenty cases personally studied by Dr. Stevenson that he believes are indicative of the reincarnation experience.

The book does not contain any cases that are ambiguous or suspicious, like that of Bridey Murphy, or dubious theories, like those of Edgar Cayce. In his studies, Dr. Stevenson does not make use of hypnotism or rely on mystical or theosophical principles. The methods he uses are empirically and scientifically impeccable, making him a powerful and convincing proponent of the theory of reincarnation.

One of Dr. Stevenson's strangest cases was that of a Lebanese boy called Imad Elawar. His family belonged to a religious sect called the Druses, who believe in the transmigration of the soul and in reincarnation. Imad was almost five years old in 1964 when Dr. Stevenson visited his village about fifteen miles east of Beirut. Since the age of two, Imad had been referring to a previous life in another village not far from his own. But although the two villages were only about twenty miles apart, they were separated by virtually impassable roads through rugged mountains. For that reason there had always been little contact between their inhabitants.

What interested Dr. Stevenson most was that Imad claimed to have lived this previous life only a few years before his present one. This made it easy to corroborate his story, since the child could name dates and the names of people who, according to him, had been members of his family as well as friends and neighbors.

Accompanied by Imad and his parents, Dr. Stevenson visited the other village. When they arrived, it was easy to find several people who could support much of Imad's information. For example, Imad claimed that his name had been Bouhamzy and that his wife had been called Jamile. One member of his family had died in a car accident. The villagers took Dr. Stevenson, Imad, and his parents to a house that had belonged to an Ibrahim Bouhamzy some ten years earlier, five years before Imad was born. Ibrahim Bouhamzy had lived with a woman called Jamile and had died of tuberculosis at the age of twenty-five. One of his cousins, named Said, had died in a car crash. All of this confirmed what Imad had said, but Dr. Stevenson was not easily convinced. He insisted in asking the child to describe the interior of the house, providing details that could not be deduced from the outside. The child proceeded to describe the house in minute details, including the toolshed and the animals' quarters. He also identified the other members of the Bouhamzy family and their neighbors, all still living and none of whom he had ever seen before.

After studying this information and questioning Imad and his parents for several weeks, Dr. Stevenson concluded that the case of Imad Elawar "suggested" the existence of reincarnation. There was no other way to explain Imad's remarkable revelations if he had not lived before as Ibrahim Bouhamzy.

Of course, there are many cases of people who claim to have lived in other times and other bodies, but none has been as carefully verified and documented as the case of Imad Elawar. Today, this continues to be one of the classic cases providing strong evidence of the survival of the personality and the mystery of reincarnation.

This leads us to ask: Is there enough evidence to prove without doubt the phenomenon of reincarnation? Unfortunately, the answer is no. The evidence exists, but it is not conclusive. Even the case of Imad Elawar can be questioned. The parents might have planned the whole thing and coached the child, who was obviously very precocious. There is no way of proving that this did not happen, despite Dr. Stevenson's belief in the veracity of all the persons involved. It was for this reason that he called his book *Twenty Cases* Suggestive *of Reincarnation,* not that they prove it beyond a reasonable doubt. This cautious approach will be found in all areas of scientific research and is essential if we are to preserve the integrity of scientific inquiry. Ultimately, it is this skepticism that frees us from superstition, ignorance, and fanaticism.

With a subject as important as reincarnation, all data must be measured and studied meticulously. There is plenty of evidence to support the theory of spiritual survival and reincarnation, but more work is necessary. There are now many laboratories, like the one in Princeton University, where scientists are conducting painstaking research on the awesome powers of the human mind and the possibility that it may survive the trauma of physical death and continue to exist in another, similar environment. This research is vital because it may ultimately provide us with the proof we seek. This proof could very well transform the way we perceive ourselves and those around us. In turn, this new perception could alter our relationships with others and with our environment. It could also affect our actions and possibly help curb antisocial behavioral patterns. Above all, it could give us a new sense of hope at a time when we often feel an increasing sense of hopelessness. This assurance of survival and rebirth must come to us through science. Faith is insufficient because it does not require proof. But when science believes in something, the whole world believes.

§

after death

what happens

**the life
of the
spirit**

what happens

after death

7 **IN THE PRECEDING CHAPTERS** we have explored strong indications that the human personality, who and what we really are, continues to exist after the death of the physical body. These indications are based on tantalizing and exciting new evidence about the survival of the spirit and its possible rebirth in another body, the phenomenon known as reincarnation. Most probably what survives is the electromagnetic energy of which our minds are made, the familiar ego with whom we identify.

We have also discussed the accounts of many people who claim to have gone through a tunnel of light during near-death experiences (NDEs), at the end of which they met an angelic or Christlike figure. In some instances, already-deceased friends and relatives met the person undergoing the NDE with the intention of guiding him or her in their new existence as a disembodied spirit. This existence takes place in the astral world, which is formed of electromagnetic vibrations of different densities and magnitudes. After death each spirit finds its own energy level according to its evolutionary state and vibratory rate. According to the people who have visited the astral realm during out-of-body or near-death experiences, there are landscapes, oceans, rivers, flora, fauna, and even buildings in this other world, the same as in the physical world because they have been created by the minds of the beings who inhabit it and who previously lived on Earth. As we saw in chapter 2, people who have had contact with astral entities through transcommunication say that these beings report that astral matter is malleable and can be mentally manipulated to take whichever form is desired.

In the astral world there are zones of great beauty and light that are occupied by higher spirits, but there are also places of darkness and terror inhabited by dark and destructive entities. These terrifying habitations have also been created by the mental vibrations and memories of the beings that inhabit them, most of whom committed terrible crimes and other destructive acts during their material lives.

As we saw in chapter 4, the inhabitants of the astral world can descend to the lower planes but are unable to ascend to the higher ones. This happens because each plane of existence in the astral world has its own vibratory rate, which is faster than the planes below it and slower than those above it. The higher a location of a plane, the faster will be its vibratory rate. The vibratory rate of a spirit depends on its evolutionary development and is in perfect harmony with the plane to which it belongs. If a spirit ascends to a superior plane, it finds that it cannot resist the stronger, faster vibrations and has to descend again to its own level. Should it descend to a lower plane, however, the slower, denser vibrations will not affect its molecular structure, and it may remain there as long as it wishes. According to most mystical schools, higher spirits descend to the lower levels of the astral plane only so that they may help the spirits who inhabit these dark regions rise above their dismal spiritual degradation and seek redemption.

So far we have been examining the possibilities of life after death based mostly on the results of various investigations into the subject or on the accounts of people who have had out-of-body or near-death experiences. Let us now consider the life of the spirit in those ultrasonic regions that lie beyond the physical world as we know it. To do this, we must perforce use speculation, but speculation based on logical assumptions.

To begin with, if the spirit is made of mental energy—in other words, if mind and spirit are one and the same thing—then it follows that what we know as spirit is very much a part of the material world. It is a physical entity, however subtle its essence might be, because energy in all its forms is part of the physical Universe. We may not be able to see a hydrogen atom, but it is still a physical quantity. We even know its actual weight.

It is obvious that the physical world is one of the most dense among the lower planes, and we can certainly agree that it is far denser than the astral plane. If spirits on higher planes can descend to those on a lower level, it would then seem quite feasible for them to descend to our material plane, to our physical reality. Swami Panchadasi and the oriental schools of mysticism tell us that the astral bodies of those who have died can remain on Earth only for a short time, but they also say that it is possible for a spirit to descend to a denser plane and remain there for a while if it so chooses. This means that after the astral body has disintegrated, the spirit, which is immortal and is the seat of consciousness, can return to Earth if it wants to. If this is so, what is to stop a maleficent spirit from returning to the material world to torment people? Likewise, good spirits could conceivably return to Earth to help and inspire loved ones and humankind in general to overcome obstacles and rise above the human condition. These rather awesome possibilities are given a stronger foundation because of the accounts of people who have had unnerving experiences with spiritual entities, some of them destructive and others of a higher, inspiring nature.

§

One of these inspiring cases is that of an Englishwoman called Rosemary Brown. In her book *Incomplete Symphonies*, she writes that when she was a young girl, she had a recurrent vision of a man in late-nineteenth-century dress. The man assured her that one day she would receive instructions on how to write classical music directly from famous composers who were dead.

Rosemary grew up and got married, but unfortunately, not long afterward her husband died and left her with two small children. Trying to survive on her own with her children proved a severe stress on Rosemary, and she experienced times of great poverty and despair. One day she passed by an antique shop and saw in the window a portrait of the man she had seen in her visions as a child. Filled with curiosity, she went inside the store and asked the owner the name of the man in the portrait. He replied that it was the famous Hungarian composer Franz Liszt.

Rosemary was profoundly impressed by the incident. She returned home as if in a trance, sat down at a table, and proceeded to trace the lines of the musical scale on a piece of paper. She then wrote a complicated sonata for the piano. Rosemary Brown is not an accomplished pianist, much less a composer. Her knowledge of the piano is very basic. Yet when she brought the composition to a music expert for analysis, he told her that it was written in the unmistakable style of Franz Liszt.

That was in 1964. Since then, Rosemary Brown has written dozens of compositions in the styles of Chopin, Beethoven, Debussy, Rachmaninoff, Brahms, Bach, and, naturally, Liszt. According to Rosemary, all of these works were dictated to her in the native language of the composers, which included Polish, French, Russian, and German. When Chopin dictated in Polish, she would write the words phonetically and then pass the material to a Polish friend, who would translate them. Rosemary's most recent work is the Tenth Symphony by Beethoven, who, as we all know, wrote only nine symphonies. The Tenth, according to Rosemary, is a grand choral work like the Ninth. She expects this massive work to take many years to complete.

In the world of classical music, there has been a mixed reaction to these "posthumous" works. Some critics say that the music is not the composers' best, being reminiscent of their better early works. But many distinguished musicians have been astounded by Rosemary's work. The pianist Hephzibah Menuhin has great respect for the compositions because in his opinion they have been written in the exact styles of the masters. The composer Richard Rodney Bennet is even more specific. It is possible to improvise, he says, but it would be impossible to create these works without many years of musical training. He goes on to say that he would be unable to duplicate the Beethoven compositions produced by Rosemary.

In a similar case, a young Brazilian painter, who works very rapidly in the dark with his eyes closed, produces paintings in the styles of Renoir, Picasso, Monet, Van Gogh, Toulouse-Lautrec, and da Vinci. Each painting is different, and each carries the personal stamp of the master, just like the compositions of Rosemary Brown.

We have previously seen that many works of art are said to be created in the astral world and later brought forth in the material world. The above cases tend to corroborate these astral concepts.

§

Another famous case that supports the continued life of the spirit after death happened in England in the 1930s after a British airship, code-named R101, crashed into a mountain range in France, instantly killing forty-eight of the fifty-four passengers. Among the dead was the airship's captain, a young navigation lieutenant called H. C. Irwin.

Two days after the tragedy, a group of spiritualists, among them a well-known psychic investigator called Harry Price and a journalist called Ian Coster, gathered in the National Laboratory for Psychic Studies with a young psychic by the name of Eileen Garrett. The researchers were trying to establish contact with Sir Arthur Conan Doyle, who fervently believed in reincarnation when he was alive. Conan Doyle, best known as the creator of Sherlock Holmes, had devoted much of his life to studying the survival of the personality and for years had tried unsuccessfully to contact the spirits of his mother and son, who had died in World War I. The researchers were convinced that if the spirit of Conan Doyle had survived the trauma of death, they would be able to contact it.

Soon after the beginning of the experiment, Eileen Garrett fell into a trance. But instead of the voice of Sir Arthur Conan Doyle, the researchers heard a very distressed voice that identified itself as Flight Lieutenant H. C.

Irwin, captain of the ill-fated dirigible R101. Speaking rapidly and in a faltering voice, Lieutenant Irwin, supposedly speaking through Eileen Garrett, proceeded to explain in detailed technical language exactly how and why the accident had occurred. With no prior knowledge of aeronautics, Eileen Garrett described in perfect detail the interior and exterior of the dirigible, its mechanical components, and gave an explicit description of the reason the dirigible had crashed.

The reporter wrote down the entire story in shorthand and published it immediately. Eventually the description of this extraordinary meeting came to the attention of one of the engineers who had built the dirigible. The engineer's name was Charlton, and he was able to verify that all the information given by Eileen Garrett while she was in the trance was not only true but also highly confidential and would have been known only by the captain and members of the team that had built the airship. In Charlton's opinion, Lieutenant Irwin had established a conscious communication through Eileen Garrett to inform the government about the problems with the craft so that a similar tragedy could be avoided. Six months later, a board of investigation found that all the information from the trance communication with Eileen Garrett was correct to the smallest detail.

This dramatic example of the possibilities of life after death established Eileen Garrett as one of the most famous psychics in the world at the time. Some years later she wrote various books about the occult, including the very popular *Telepathy* and *Adventures in the Supernatural*.

§

Among the notable scientists who have tried to find proof that the personality survives death was Thomas Alva Edison, inventor of the lightbulb and the phonograph. Edison was convinced that there was a frequency somewhere between long and short wave that would allow us to communicate directly with the astral world. For many years he tried to invent a machine that would provide that link but was unsuccessful in this work. Guglielmo Marconi, inventor of the radio, was another scientist who worked secretly on a machine that would let him receive messages from the past. A devout Catholic, Marconi was hoping to hear the last words of Jesus on the cross.

In chapter 2 we talked of voices of the dead recorded on tape and on television. As we saw in that chapter, one of the pioneers in this field was a Russian-born Swedish film producer called Friedrich Jurgenson. For several years, Jurgenson had been recording the sounds of forest birds in Sweden. Returning home one day after a session in the woods, Jurgenson heard not the sounds of the birds but the voice of his deceased mother saying, "Friedel, my little Friedel, can you hear me?" Dumbfounded, Jurgenson played back the recording and again heard the voice of his mother, who had been dead a long time. He began a long series of experiments during which he recorded hundreds of voices that appeared mysteriously on his magnetic tapes. Around 1967, Pope Paul VI learned of the Swede's experiments, and it was rumored that the Vatican was taking a great interest in Jurgenson's voices from the astral world.

When Jurgenson's work became known, other investigators began new and different experiments. Among them was Latvian psychologist Dr. Konstantin Raudive, whose messages from the beyond we discussed in chapter 2. Raudive used new and very sensitive instruments in his research. In 1968, he recorded over 70,000 voices that, according to him, had originated in the beyond. His work gained such prominence that eventually all recordings of supernatural voices became known as "Raudive voices." Raudive said that anyone can conduct similar experiments, using a sensitive instrument to record the simple sounds of nature, such as birdcalls, the sound of river water, thunderstorms, or the seashore. Later on, one may find mixed with natural sounds the echoes of another, quite surreal world.

Among some of the famous voices that Raudive is said to have recorded were those of Churchill, Tolstoy, Hitler, Nietzsche, Kennedy, and Stalin. Most of the messages were short, and nearly all alluded to the survival of the spirit. "The dead live, Konstantin," "We exist, Konstantin," and "Please, believe it," are examples of typical messages received by the Latvian psychologist.

In the 1970s, an English student called David Ellis received a grant to study the voices recorded by Dr. Raudive. Ellis concluded that the voices were legitimate, but he also said that Raudive might have created them in his own mind. The possibility that these were the voices of spirits inhabiting the astral world, although probably true, was one David Ellis could not verify.

It's obvious from the evidence we have already seen that there is enough knowledge to support the possibility that some part of the personality or spirit of an individual survives physical death. There also is evidence that would support the theory that these spirits can try to make contact with people still living on Earth. Among the types of possible contact are voice recordings. However, there are also cases where normal people without much psychic knowledge have seen the physical form of a person who has died.

§

Several years ago, an unexplainable event took place in my home town of Arecibo, Puerto Rico. Arecibo is a very small town, typical of so many tropical hamlets in the Caribbean islands, but it has a history deeply steeped in eerie legends and strange happenings. Even the terrain is unusual, with a very large and rugged karstic countryside, one of the largest in the world. In one of these nature's potholes, Cornell University built the well-known Arecibo Ionospheric Observatory, where the world's scientific community awaits extraterrestrial contact. The event I refer to is the most impressive example I know of actual physical contact with the dead. It is a real ghost story.

One of the best-known families in Arecibo had an only daughter who had recently married and was living at home with her new husband. At the time of the story, the daughter was twenty-five years old and worked in the neighboring town of Aguadilla, about an hour's drive from Arecibo. She drove to work every morning and returned home around six in the evening. One rainy afternoon as she was driving back, she lost control of the car, crashed into a tree on the side of the road, and was killed instantly. Her death devastated her parents and her young husband. A house that had once been happy and full of laughter became suddenly silent and filled with grief.

Several months later, around six in the evening, a man was driving his taxi on the highway between Aguadilla and

Arecibo. It had been a quiet day, and he hadn't had many fares. As he passed the tree where the accident had happened, a young woman seemed to appear from nowhere and flagged him down. The driver stopped, hoping that he would finally be able to earn some money. The girl got into the car and asked to be taken to Arecibo. The taxi driver refused at first because he did not want to drive so far, but after being promised a large tip, he agreed to take the girl to Arecibo.

There was no conversation during the journey, and when they arrived at their destination, the girl directed the driver to a large, elegant villa in a wealthy area of town. When they arrived, the girl asked the driver to wait, as she had to go inside and get the money she had promised him. The driver was not at all suspicious and settled down to wait. He watched the girl climb the stairs leading to a wide verandah and disappear into the house.

Time passed, and the young woman did not return. Finally the driver began to get impatient and a little worried. Suspecting that he might have been the victim of a common scam, he finally decided to knock on the house's door. Almost at once the door was opened by a pale, sad-faced young man. The taxi driver explained what had happened and demanded that the girl be called, as he wanted to be paid for his services. When the young man said that nobody had come into the house, the indignant driver felt sure they were trying to cheat him out of his fare and threatened to call the police.

Suddenly, the young man turned even paler and asked the taxi driver to come inside the house and wait for a few minutes. The suspicious driver agreed but told him not to take too long. After a few minutes, the man returned with a photograph of a girl and asked the driver, "Is this the young lady who asked to be brought to this house?"

"That's her, I'll swear it on my mother," answered the driver.

"This is my wife," said the young man, "who was killed six months ago in a car accident at the same place where you picked her up."

When he heard this, the driver began to shake uncontrollably and fell in a dead faint to the floor. He spent several days in the hospital because of the severe shock that the experience had on his nervous system.

§

If Panchadasi is correct, the entities that make themselves visible in cases like this are really the astral bodies of people who have died a short time before. However, many cases are also reported of similar materializations concerning people who have been dead for many years. According to the traditional teachings we have discussed in this book, the astral bodies of those people should have disintegrated within months or at most a few years after death. So if it is true that these manifestations took place, what or who produced the manifestations and how? Was the physical contact made by the disembodied personality of the dead person? In the Arecibo story, how were the visible materialization and the actual voice and speech of the dead girl accomplished?

If the spirits that inhabit the astral world can establish contact with the material world, then it is also possible for our thoughts and actions to be constantly influenced by these disembodied entities, a very disturbing idea for every human being who wants to be in complete control of his or her life. Furthermore, this influence could be positive or negative depending on the evolutionary level of the spirit in question. For this reason, most of the religious and mystical schools teach us that each time we have to face an important decision, we should ensure that the final decision is made by us, by our personal convictions, and that we should avoid impulsive actions that could be the result of outside spiritual influences.

Based on the scientific evidence and the psychic experiences that we have examined so far, we can speculate the following:

> It is very probable that when a person dies, his or her instincts and emotions, what is known as the astral body, survive for a short time together with some of the individual's memories and basic personality traits. Later, this astral body disintegrates slowly. In the meantime, the conscious personality or ego, what is known as the spirit, rests for a specific period of time in the astral world, and then it passes on to the appropriate mental or astral level, depending on its state of evolution. There it lives, works, and sometimes creates works of art, often similar to those it accomplished while in the world of matter. These works sometimes become manifest in the physical world by human beings who labor under the direct influence of a disembodied spirit. Rosemary Brown's music work is an example of such an influence.
>
> From the mental or astral world, the spirit, once it has awakened from its restful sleep, can descend, if it so wishes, to lower levels, including the material or Earth plane. It cannot, however,

ascend to higher levels than its own, which may
be possible only after a spirit has advanced in
its evolutionary path and has reached the higher
spiritual planes. Generally, spirits descend to the
material level with the intention of influencing
human beings. This influence can be either posi-
tive or negative, depending on the evolutionary
development of the spirit.

In the astral world, the spirit lives a life as
solid and real as we do in the material world
because each being, whether physical or spiri-
tual, tends to identify with the plane it inhabits.
Because that plane is formed of the same vibra-
tions as those of the beings that dwell therein, its
inhabitants perceive such a plane as true reality.

The mysterious and unfathomable astral world is revealed to us in all its splendor during our dream lives. That
is why the phantasmagorical world of dreams seems so real
to us when we sleep. We are simply traveling in our spirit
body in the astral world, where the spirit truly belongs.
When we dream, we are moving through the various subplanes of the astral world, where we can have exhilarating
or terrifying experiences. Only when we have lucid dreams,
and we are fully aware that we are dreaming, are we able to
control the malleable stuff of which the astral world is
made and manipulate the dream or astral experience at
will. That is why it is so very important to learn the art of
lucid dreaming: If we are able to separate the dream state
from the world of physical reality, we would also be able to
recognize the moment of final separation of the spirit from
the material body at the moment of death.

The ancients taught that the life of the spirit in the astral world is the true life and that life in the physical plane is only a theater, a learning experience, a short sojourn, a kind of pilgrimage that the spirit makes for a determined period of time, at the end of which it returns to its true home, the astral world.

§

after death

what happens

spiritual archetypes

what happens

after death

8 THE CONCEPT OF ARCHETYPES

was introduced to the language of psychology by the great Swiss psychoanalyst Carl Gustav Jung, who also coined the term *unconscious* to denote the content of the human psyche. According to Jung, the unconscious is formed of various archetypes, each of which represents, and at the same time controls, an aspect of the personality.

Each archetype is a concentration of psychic energy, identified by Jung as libido. This energy or libido is manifested as the various archetypes or separate entities composing each individual personality.

Among the archetypes described by Jung as integral parts of the personality or psyche are the following: the Ego, or conscious personality; the Superego, which is the idealistic part of the psyche; the Shadow, formed by the concentration of all the uncontrolled, and often destructive, instincts of the individual; the Anima, or feminine aspect of the psyche in a man; the Animus, or masculine aspect of the psyche in a woman; the Amazon, or concentration of intellectual power; the Magician, or concentration of spiritual power; the Great Mother, symbol of maternal instincts; the Old Man, symbol of paternal instincts; and others of lesser importance individually, but nevertheless vital when considering the whole of the personality.

Each archetype is a different aspect of the personality ideally functioning in perfect balance with the other archetypes. Any disharmony among the archetypes can lead to mental or psychic imbalances of the personality. The average person generally has a reasonable balance among the various archetypes of his or her unconscious. When one archetype tends to dominate the others, the person develops mental or nervous disturbances, nightmares, fears, insecurities, and depression.

Besides these archetypes of the unconscious, there are also universal archetypes generally identified with historical and religious figures, legendary heroes, and supernatural beings like angels, fairies, gnomes, sirens, and the gods and goddesses of various world mythologies. These also play an important role in the content of the human psyche.

According to Jung, the combined psychic energies of all the unconscious minds of the entire human race form a unified whole that he calls the collective unconscious, which is like a vast mental pool where all human minds or psyches may eventually meet or merge. When asleep or unconscious, or simply daydreaming, a person's unconscious mind may descend into the collective unconscious to rest or to gather new energies. It is possible at this time for people who know each other to establish contact at an unconscious level. This contact surfaces in the conscious personality in the form of a dream or of memories of the other person. This explains many cases known as telepathy or clairvoyance, when someone dreams about another person and then meets him in the street or receives a telephone call from him.

When an archetype is formulated in the collective unconscious of the human race, it becomes one of the archetypes that make up each individual mind or psyche, regardless of ethnic origin. For example, when Jesus was globally perceived as the redeemer of the Christian world, he eventually came to exist in this manner in the collective mind of humanity not only among Christians but also among Jews, Muslims, Hindus, and others who do not believe in or practice Christianity. This does not mean that non-Christians accept Jesus as the redeemer of the world. What it means is that the telesmatic image of Jesus and his religious significance exists in all human psyches because it is by now part of the collective unconscious of the entire human race.

The telesmatic image is a symbol or figure that comprises all the characteristics of the archetype. The telesmatic image of Jesus, or Christ figure, is universally perceived as a young man with a chestnut beard and shoulder-length hair, dressed in a robe and mantle, wearing sandals and displaying open wounds on the palms of his hands. The figure has a gentle expression and is surrounded by a brilliant halo of light. The typical telesmatic image of an angel, on the other hand, generally appears dressed in white with wavy fair hair, large white wings, and Roman sandals. The well-known angels, like Michael, Raphael, or Gabriel, have been assigned specific colors and certain attributes by popular religiosity, and that is how their special telesmatic images are perceived and recognized. Michael, for example, is generally represented dressed in red and green Roman armor, sword in hand, his sandaled foot pressed against the devil's neck. Raphael, on the other hand, is usually envisioned carrying a fish in one hand (a symbol of his adventures with Tobias) and dressed in robes of yellow and violet.

Some archetypes are more recent than others. Jesus, the Buddha, Zoroaster, and the figures of the saints are historical concepts from definite time periods. Others, like the angels and archangels, although known by ancient civilizations such as the Babylonians and the Hebrews, are cosmic concepts whose real origin is unknown.

Another archetype of the universal cosmic order is the Virgin Mary. Like Jesus, Mary has a historical identity, and her origin can be traced to a definite time period, but her identification with the concepts of the universal mother and the perfect woman transform her into a cosmic archetype. Her essence transcends her human origins and is linked with the feminine aspect of God, the Divine Mother, the Matrona, and the Holy Spirit. In this sense, Mary's archetypal importance transcends that of Jesus himself.

These religious images—Jesus, the Virgin Mary, the angels, and the saints—are among the more important universal archetypes. In syncretic religions like Afro-Cuban Santería, where many Catholic saints have been identified with the orishas of the Yoruba religion, the saints as well as the orishas have separate identities. The orisha Chango, for example, is usually identified with St. Barbara but has his own telesmatic image where he is represented as an African king with beautiful features, dressed in red and white, wearing a crown shaped like a tower and encrusted with cowrie shells, and clutching in one hand a double-edged ax. The image of St. Barbara, on the other hand, is that of a virginal adolescent dressed in white robes and a red mantle. Her gold crown is also shaped like a tower, and a tower reposes at her feet. In one hand she holds a sword and in the other, a gold goblet. So while Chango and St. Barbara have different telesmatic images, they share several of the same attributes. That is the reason why their archetypes, while apparently different, are formed by the same psychic energies and respond to the same human perception.

Religious archetypes provide the kind of psychic energy that Jung called libido and that in Santería is known as ashe. It makes little difference what this energy is called. What matters is to recognize that it is the primeval substance from which everything that exists was created and the basis for all that exists. This psychic energy is necessary to make life and living possible, for without it, there can be no existence or awareness of existence as we know it.

Each religious archetype contains a great concentration of this energy, and to tap into it, one must open the door behind which lurks the archetype whose specific energy we need or desire. Once we acquire the energy, we must merge with it and harmonize it within our conscious, everyday personality in order to acquire the things that particular energy or archetype represents. If we are unable to balance this new energy into our conscious personality, grave disturbances may take place around the individual—not only mental or spiritual, but also of a very physical nature. There are many religious and magical rituals, each designed for the purpose of releasing psychic energies into the human personality. Without the correct transmutation of these archetypal forces, much damage can be done to the conscious personality, and very real and undesirable phenomena may suddenly appear in the life of the individual.

It is important to remember that each archetype controls a different aspect of human life. Earlier in this chapter, I mentioned personal archetypes like the Ego, the Superego, the Shadow, and various others. Then I described the universal archetypes, among which are found the religious telesmatic images. Each of these archetypes controls a certain area of human interest.

The archangel Michael, for example, is a symbol of justice and control over evil. When help is needed in these matters, this archangel is often petitioned or invoked through religious or magical rituals. In love problems, the various Catholic archetypes that can be invoked include St. Anthony, St. Elena, and St. Martha. In Haitian Voodun, the loa Erzulie is propitiated for the same reason; in Santería, they invoke the orisha Oshun; and in ritual magic, the invoked force is the archangel Anael, regent of the sphere of Venus, long associated with love. Regardless of the archetype invoked, the type of energy involved is the same. The more powerful the archetype, and the stronger the contact, the higher will be the concentration of energy released by the unconscious mind. How the energy received is used and balanced is what will determine the eventual outcome of the psychic contact.

§

It is not easy to contact the desired archetype, but once contact is made and the door is open, the archetype's energy flows, and the desired result may be achieved. It is not only difficult to make contact with an archetype but also to use only the necessary energy to achieve what is wanted. In situations where the libido or psychic energy has not been properly balanced and the door or split in the archetype has remained open, the uncontrolled outpouring of archetypal energy becomes a powerful part of the stream of consciousness of the individual, overpowering the conscious personality to such an extent as to create a psychosis or mental imbalance.

A typical example of this type of unchecked archetypal energy overpowering the personality is that of German philosopher Friedrich Nietzsche, who decided to experiment with the universal archetype known as Zoroaster. Eventually, this released archetype controlled Nietzsche so completely that he became convinced that he was Zoroaster and ended by committing suicide. One could say that the psychic energy expressed as the archetype Zoroaster was released from Nietzsche's unconscious with such force that Nietzsche was unable to control or stop its flow until it totally overwhelmed the other archetypal energies, throwing Nietzsche's personality out of balance and eventually destroying him.

This case exemplifies Jung's contention that the various archetypes must be perfectly balanced within the conscious personality. When an individual has finally accomplished this task, it is said in Jungian terms that the person has completed an individuation process.

The overpowering of the conscious personality by a given archetype is known as possession. This outpouring of psychic energies is safe under certain circumstances. This happens when the archetype possessing an individual is identified with that person's Superego, which is the highest aspect of the unconscious mind. In Santería, where possession is very common, the archetype who is identified with the Superego is known as that person's guardian angel, or eledda, and is said to govern or direct the person and to be the person's mother or father, depending on the archetype or orisha involved. Each guardian angel is identified with one of the orishas or saints. A son or daughter of Eleggua can be possessed by this orisha or saint without endangering the personality. While possessed in this manner the person loses all individuality and acts as if he or she were Eleggua. This happens because the psychic energy that forms the archetype known as Eleggua rushes forth from the unconscious and overpowers the conscious personality of the individual possessed—at that moment, that person *is* Eleggua.

The easiest and most common form of possession takes place during the playing of the ritual drums in Santería. Each orisha has his or her own distinctive drum rhythms that during ritual dancing can place sensitive individuals in a light, semihypnotic trance. It is during this trance state that most possessions take place, as each drum rhythm allows a person to go deep into his or her unconscious, releasing the archetypal energies of the Superego or orisha with whom that person is identified.

The reason why an orisha like Eleggua can possess a person without creating a mental schism, such as the one experienced by Nietzsche with Zoroaster, is that in Santería the psyche or mind of an initiate is prepared beforehand to be able to withstand the power of the released energies of his or her ruling orisha or Superego without harm to the conscious personality. The archetypal energies released during possession are then absorbed and harmoniously balanced into the individual's consciousness.

There are only two orishas who can possess any human mind in the Santería tradition. Their names are Obatalá and Babalú-Ayé. They represent peace and well-being, respectively, although Babalú-Ayé also represents illness and pestilence in his darker aspects. In other words, peace and well-being as archetypes are always allowed to take over the personality because in essence they cannot harm it. In fact, the conscious personality can only benefit from their archetypal energies. But for the most part, each person is said to be ruled by a specific orisha or archetypal force, which is generally the only one that takes possession of that individual's personality.

The preparation of a person's mind to absorb the archetypal energies of his or her Superego or ruling orisha takes place during the person's initiation into the mysteries of that particular orisha or saint. Even so, when possession takes place, the person acts as if he or she had received a powerful electric jolt and often goes into convulsions similar to an epileptic seizure. Apparently this happens because large quantities of psychic energy are released at that moment into the conscious personality, which is then totally eclipsed by the personality of the archetype.

In the practice of Spiritism, which we will discuss in some detail in the next chapter, there is a belief in spirit guides and spiritual teachers. Among the spirit guides are a great number of archetypes like the Madama, the Gypsy, the American Indian, the Pirate, the Arab, the Hindu, the African, the Nun, and many others. Many of those who practice Spiritism believe firmly that their principal guide is one of these archetypes.

The archetype known as the Madama is one of the more popular guides in Spiritism. She is characterized as a heavy black woman dressed in white with a white handkerchief tied around her head. She is often described as carrying a straw basket filled with fresh plants. She is very friendly and happy and speaks with a heavy African accent whenever she manifests through possession.

The psychic energy that forms the various archetypes is neutral, but within the unconscious there are positive and negative instincts that help shape the personality of each archetype. So there are positive archetypes, like the orishas and the Madama, and negative archetypes, representing humanity's destructive instincts. In Spiritism, the latter are identified with what are known as lower or less-evolved spirits. There is a continual battle between these good and evil spirits, symbolizing the struggle within each individual to control his or her destructive impulses and to maximize the good and creative side of the personality. This constant struggle between the emerging positive and negative archetypal energies of the human psyche is at the core of the beliefs and practices of Spiritism.

§

after death

what happens

spiritualism and spiritism

what happens

after death

9 IN 1744, SWEDISH SCIENTIST and mystic Emmanuel Swedenborg began to write extensively about the spirit world and the revelations he allegedly received from saints, angels, and other high spirits who communicated with him through dreams and visions. Often Swedenborg found himself wandering in other worlds, where he was counseled and instructed by the spirits of long-dead kings, popes, and various biblical figures.

Swedenborg was not the only famous scientist who believed in the life of the spirit or in mysticism. René Descartes, Isaac Newton, and Benjamin Franklin all shared these ideas. It was Swedenborg's experience, shared through his writings, that aroused European interest in life after death and introduced a new concept of the nature of personality survival.

Before Swedenborg, the popular Christian belief was that after death the soul went directly to either heaven or hell or, if you were Catholic, to purgatory. The life of the spirit in these unknown regions was portrayed as being totally different from life in the material world. According to Swedenborg's ideas, which revolutionized the view of life after death in his time, life in the spirit world is very similar to life in the material world. His conversations with the souls of the departed indicated that communication was possible between the physical and the spiritual worlds.

About seventy-five years after Swedenborg's death, a humble cobbler's apprentice had a vision in which Swedenborg and the Greek physician Galen talked to him about the existence of life after death. This man, named Andrew Jackson Davis, despite being only eighteen years old and having little formal education, began to write erudite works on the supernatural powers of the human body that he called magnetism and electricity. In 1845, he went into a trance and began to dictate a voluminous work entitled *The Principles of Nature, Its Divine Revelations and the Voice of Humanity*, in which he made the following prediction:

> *It is certain that spirits communicate with each other in spite of the fact that some are confined in human form and some are in the superior planes. It is also certain that very soon physical evidence will be provided to attest to these truths. When this happens, the world will accept enthusiastically the beginning of a new era in which the truth about the life of the spirit will be revealed.*

Three years later, on March 31, 1848, Davis said that he felt a warm breath on his neck and heard a soft voice say to him, "Brother, the work has begun. The first physical demonstration has been received."

This happened in the town of Poughkeepsie, New York. That same day, in the nearby village of Hydesville, three young girls called Margaret, Kate, and Leah Fox were playing in the house where they lived with their parents. Margaret was ten years old, Leah was nine, and Kate was barely seven.

For several days, the Fox family had been hearing a series of mysterious rappings coming from one of the walls of their house. On March 31, the same day Davis received the strange message, the sisters decided to establish a communication with whom they thought was a spirit making the eerie sounds.

Kate, the youngest, asked the entity to repeat her actions and then proceeded to clap her hands. Almost at once, there were several taps on the wall imitating the sound made by Kate. Then Margaret, wanting to join the fun, asked the entity to count to four. Immediately there were four consecutive taps on the wall. The girls were so frightened that they ran from the room. After a while, they returned with Leah, the third sister, and the three girls established the first series of spiritual communications in recent history.

The girls invented a system of questions and answers to communicate with the spirit. Through this system they learned that during his lifetime the entity had been a dealer in iron scraps and that he had been murdered and buried under the foundations of the house. Nearly fifty years later, an excavation under the house was undertaken to verify the sisters' claims. The remains of a man, apparently murdered, were found amid the house foundations, together with the tools of an ironmonger.

§

The experiences of the Fox sisters, predicted by Andrew Jackson Davis, marked the birth of what would eventually become known as Spiritualism. The sisters became mediums of international fame, and Spiritualism spread like wildfire throughout the United States and Europe. On the

European continent, the practice of communicating with spirits became extremely fashionable, and large numbers of mediums seemed to materialize from nowhere, all of them alleging to possess extraordinary gifts to communicate with the dead. Many of these were obvious frauds, but there were some among them who displayed unusual talents for spirit communication that could not be easily explained.

Among the most famous mediums of the time was an Englishman called Daniel Dunglas Home, who could levitate his body several feet off the floor, sometimes touching the ceiling with his head. Home would not only levitate; when he entered a room, it would shake as if in the throes of an earthquake. Ghostly hands would appear to close his eyes, and his communications with the spirits were extremely accurate. During one of the sessions, a witness said that he saw Home grow a foot taller while keeping his feet on the ground. Among the famous people who consulted with Homes on a regular basis were the English poet Elizabeth Barrett Browning and the French emperor Napoleon III.

In 1861, shortly after the death of Prince Albert, royal consort to Queen Victoria, a thirteen-year-old boy called Robert James Lees fell into a trance during a Spiritualist meeting in his house. While Lees was in this trance a spirit claiming to be Prince Albert asked if he could speak to the Queen. One of those present at the meeting was a reporter for a London newspaper, who published the spirit's request the next day. The article came to the attention of Queen Victoria, who immediately dispatched two members of her court to attend a meeting at the house of Robert James Lees. During the second meeting, the spirit of Prince Albert, speaking through Lees, claimed to recognize the two court members and greeted them with their correct names, ignoring the fact that they were using false names. This time the spirit dictated a letter to the Queen using a secret name that only she knew. These events so impressed Queen Victoria that she ordered young Mr. Lees to come to the palace so that she might talk with Prince Albert through him. Robert lived in the palace for a short time, but then, just as suddenly as it had appeared, the spirit left and apparently decided to talk to the Queen through a stable hand at Balmoral Castle in Scotland. This man, John Brown, became a personal lackey of the Queen. He was said to have been a very talented medium who served Queen Victoria for many years as a communications portal to her beloved Albert.

While Robert James Lees was working as a medium for the Queen of England, in the United States, President Abraham Lincoln was also influenced by Spiritualism.

According to a now-famous story related by Colonel Simon F. Kase, who moved at the time in the highest government circles in the United States, President Lincoln was a frequent visitor to Spiritualist meetings. During one of these reunions, a young medium called Nettie Colburn Maynard fell into a trance under the influence of a spirit who identified itself as belonging to one of the angelical orders. While under the apparent influence of this spirit the young medium approached Lincoln and began to speak about the importance of the emancipation of the slaves. According to the spirit, the Civil War would not end until the slaves were free because God had decreed that all human beings should be free. Colonel Kase, who was present at this meeting, wrote in a book that he wrote about the subject that the medium expressed herself very convincingly and intelligently, using arguments that could not possibly have been formulated by a person as young as Nettie.

Two nights later, during a second session, Lincoln was confronted by the same spirit bearing a similar message and urging the President to release the slaves. At the beginning of the Civil War, Lincoln had no intention of releasing the slaves; but in September 1862, about eight months after receiving the spirit's messages through Nettie, the President signed the Emancipation Proclamation, giving four million slaves their freedom. While the history books will not verify this information, a short time after the slaves were freed, the Civil War ended, just as the spirit had predicted.

§

At this time, Spiritualism was characterized by demonstrations made by mediums who claimed to have special abilities for contacting the spirits of the dead and, in some cases, for helping people communicate with their friends and family who had passed away. Mediums came to be known as "horses" or "houses" of the spirits, since the spirit would "ride" or "inhabit" the body of the medium during these sessions.

The Spiritualist meetings, or séances, would begin with all members of the group sitting around a round table holding hands. Generally the room was dark, since it was believed that strong light might distract the medium while in a trance.

During a routine séance, mediums would provide several proofs of their abilities. Among these demonstrations were ringing bells and the sounds of flutes, tambourines, and other musical instruments. Some mediums, like the well-known Daniel Dunglas Home, would levitate, transport chairs and tables through the air, and produce phantasmagorical hands and other phosphorescent images. One of his most popular demonstrations was the floating trumpet that would play by itself, without Homes touching it.

But undoubtedly the most spectacular act of the mediums was the emission of the mysterious substance called ectoplasm, which issued from the mouth or the solar plexus of the trance medium. Ectoplasm was described by those who saw it as a vaporous mist and was hugely popular for many years until it was proven to be a fraud perpetrated by the mediums who claimed to emit it.

Admission to these highly entertaining Spiritualist séances was not free, and the amount charged depended on the medium's reputation. Unfortunately for these mediums, growing technological developments made most of their tricks easy to expose. Eventually, all physical demonstrations at séances ceased, and the mental medium began to take center stage. The mental medium claims to establish direct contact with the spirits and can make revelations to those present at the séance on matters that only they know.

Around 1850, a Frenchman called Hippolyte Leon Denizard Rivail began an in-depth study of the beliefs and practices of Spiritualism. With the aid of ten mediums, Rivail established contact with a number of different spirit guides and asked them about life after death and the laws of the cosmos. The answers were analyzed and presented to the public in a book called *The Book of the Spirits*, which Rivail wrote under the pseudonym Allan Kardec. In this book, the French scholar included 1,018 questions and answers about creation, the life of the spirit, spiritual evolution, and reincarnation. According to Allen Kardec, not only do spirits reincarnate, they also progress and evolve, moving on to higher, more spiritually and technologically advanced planes. The beliefs of Allan Kardec became known as Spiritism.

One of the most important beliefs of Spiritism is that charity is essential for the salvation of the soul. The most charitable act that exists is giving health, whether physical, mental, or spiritual, to another person. For that reason, the driving force behind the Spiritist medium is to do acts of charity, especially spiritual healings.

After his great success with *The Book of the Spirits,* Kardec wrote other books of equal importance, such as *The Gospel According to Spiritism* and *A Collection of Chosen Prayers.* Many of these prayers are so popular in Latin America that millions of people can recite them from memory.

According to Kardec, spiritual progress is possible only through a series of progressive reincarnations. One of his basic beliefs is that God assigns a group of spirit guides to every human being upon birth. These are highly evolved entities whose work is to protect and help people with their spiritual advancement. Many of these spirit guides are believed to have been dead members of a person's family in his or her present existence or maybe even an earlier one.

Kardec insisted that it was important to communicate with these highly evolved spirits in order to receive their help in the solution to our human problems. To achieve this he began by adapting some of the principles of Spiritism to those of Christianity. Later he wrote a series of prayers and commentaries, all of which were based on a very strict moral code and ethical behavior. These teachings were later incorporated into his books. One of the many famous believers in Spiritism was French astronomer Camille Flammarion, several of whose poems were included in Kardec's *A Collection of Chosen Prayers.*

Kardec's brand of Spiritualism was more concerned with the spiritual evolution of humanity and the observation of divine laws than the original form of Spiritualism, which was more interested in the commercialization of the alleged mystical powers of the mediums. That is why he chose to make a distinction between the two by calling his teachings Spiritism.

The books of Allan Kardec had such an impact in Europe that they were quickly translated into several languages, including Spanish and Portuguese. In spite of the strict ban imposed by the Catholic Church on Kardec's books, his writings were introduced through contraband in Latin America—especially Argentina, Brazil, Cuba, Puerto Rico, and other countries in the Caribbean basin—toward the end of the nineteenth century. The practice of Spiritism quickly spread throughout these countries and soon was practiced in other Latin American countries as well. Today, Argentina and Brazil have the largest concentrations of Spiritists in the world, while about ninety percent of the inhabitants of the countries along the Caribbean basin are fervent believers in Kardec's teachings.

§

after death

what happens

incognito

what happens

after death

10 **I**N THE 1970S, TWO AMERICAN investigators traveled to Russia to study the development of extrasensory perception (ESP) among the Russians. The result of their research was a popular book entitled *PSI, Psychic Discoveries Behind the Iron Curtain.* The writers, Sheila Ostrander and Lynn Shroeder, explained that to the Russians the word psychic was interpreted not as supernatural or spiritual but rather as relating to mental powers.

The book explored how the Russians developed and used ESP and was an instant bestseller. The researchers explained that certain waves emitted by the brain are responsible for the phenomena of telepathy, clairvoyance, and other mental powers. These waves are known in neurology as Psi waves and are said to be emitted by the brain when we think. These same waves were described by Ostrander and Shroeder as responsible for telepathic communication, often unconsciously, without the individual being aware that such a communication was taking place. Psi waves are compared to radio waves because they are both long waves in terms of the electromagnetic spectrum. On the other hand, alpha waves have been detected emanating from the brain when a person is in a deep trance or in deep meditation. The onset of sleep, just before one falls asleep, is also known to take place in the alpha state.

Among the psychic practices of the Russians, Ostrander and Shroeder found the use of acupuncture, telepathy, clairvoyance, and the use of the human aura in healing. The aura is identified with the electromagnetic field that surrounds all living things. In the beginning of this century, an English physician called Dr. Walter Kilner, who at the time worked at St. Thomas's Hospital in London, discovered he could see the human aura by looking at a person through a glass screen stained with dicyanin dye. He also discovered that fatigue, disease, or changes in mood could change the color and the shape of the aura, which was also affected by magnetism, hypnosis, and electricity. Dr. Kilner went on to develop an entire system for diagnosing illness from the aura. This type of research is still being conducted in Europe and throughout the world.

Dr. Kilner's studies on the human aura influenced the Russians in their own research. Ostrander and Shroeder reported in their book that the study of the aura was not a field left in Russia to mystics and psychics, but that Russia's most learned scientists from the prestigious Presidium of the Academy of Sciences were the ones most actively investigating the phenomenon.

In the late 1940s, a husband-and-wife team made an astonishing discovery that further showed the human body emits a form of radiation that can be identified with the concept of the aura. The couple, Semyon and Valentina Kirlian, created a new method of photography with high frequency electrical fields. This type of photography used a specially constructed high-frequency spark generator, or oscillator, that could generate 75,000 to 200,000 electrical oscillations per second. The generator was connected to various clamps, plates, optical instruments, and microscopes.

A camera was unnecessary for the photographic process. The object to be "photographed" was simply inserted between the clamps of the generator along with photo paper. The generator was then switched on, creating a high-frequency field between the clamps. This caused the object held by the clamps to radiate a type of bioluminescence onto the photo paper.

The Kirlians discovered that objects photographed in this manner displayed a sort of radiation field around them. A leaf, for instance, would show bright color patterns in shades of turquoise and reddish yellow around its edges. A human hand, however, resembled a composite photograph of the Milky Way. There were multicolored flashes of light against a background of blue and gold. Some of these lights glowed steadily while others sparkled at intervals or flared brightly like Roman candles. Most importantly, the two researchers discovered that inorganic objects, like stones, metal, or rubber, showed completely different structural patterns than living things. Organic subjects, like a leaf or a hand, displayed millions of sparkling lights around and within them, while nonliving tissue showed only an even glow around the edge.

As the Kirlians advanced in their research, they discovered that high-frequency photographs could detect illness on a subject long before its onset made its appearance in the organism itself. The subject being photographed showed dark geometrical patterns along its surface shortly before an illness was diagnosed. The tests showed similar results on leaves and humans. The extraordinary conclusion reached by the Kirlians was that living things seem to have two bodies. One is the physical body, and the other is an energy field shown by the high-frequency photographs.

Incredibly, the physical body seemed to be a "mirror" of the energy body, reflecting somehow what was happening in this radiant "double" days after it happened. It looked as if the radiant or energy body was a blueprint of the physical body, which simply followed the patterns established by its subtle double.

The implication of the Kirlian team's discovery was not lost on Russian scientists, who began to study the controversial photography as soon as it was made public. But it was not until 1968, nearly twenty years after the Kirlian's initial discovery, that Russian scientists acknowledged their pioneering work. In a paper published by the State University at Kazakhstan entitled *The Biological Essence of the Kirlian Effect*, Drs. V. Inyushin et al. announced their discovery that all living things—plants, animals, and humans—have not only a physical body made of atoms and molecules but also a counterpoint body of energy they called the Biological Plasma Body. Their research further determined that the bioluminescence shown in the Kirlian photographs was caused by the bioplasma of the organism, not its electrical state. This vibrating energy has a specific spatial organization; in other words, it has shape. It also has its own internal processes that are absolutely different from the pattern of energy in the physical body. This energy body is also polarized and is specific for each organism, which is what determines the form of the organism. In other words, the energy body gives form and direction to its physical counterpart. It is clear, then, that the bioplasma body is the real person or organism.

An interesting fact also uncovered by the Kirlians is that if part of the physical body of a living thing is cut away, the bioplasma body still remains intact, clearly visible in the high-frequency photographs. But when the energy body disappears, the organism dies. This makes it imperative for the organism to replenish and nourish its energy body if it wishes to stay alive.

But how can this be accomplished? The Kazakh scientists discovered that it is the oxygen we breathe that converts some of its surplus electrons and certain quantity of energy into the energy body. Breathing seems to charge the bioplasma body, renewing our reserves of vital energy and balancing disturbed energy patterns. They also discovered that each color has a distinct influence on the energy body, changing its activity and oscillation patterns. Blue, for example, seemed to intensify the discharge of luminosity in the energy body. They also found that weak magnetic fields stabilized the luminosity.

The bioplasma or energy body discovered fortuitously by the Kirlians with their high-frequency photography and later verified by the Kazakh scientists seems to agree with the concept of the human aura that had already been observed by Dr. Kilner in the beginning of the century. The fact that the bioplasma body seems to be energized by the intake of oxygen also agrees with the practices of the special breathing known as pranayama by the yogis, who believe that there is a substance called prana in the oxygen we breathe. This prana is the essence of life, and it is what vitalizes the aura as well as the physical body.

When a person dies, the aura is dispersed, and with it the human spirit or consciousness. That is the teaching of yoga and of many other spiritual systems. According to the evidence of Kirlian photography and the biological evidence presented by the scientists from Kazakh State University, something very similar happens to the bioplasma or energy body upon death. Are the energy body and the aura the same thing?

Long before the invention of Kirlian photography and the verification of its findings by Inyushin et al., many European and American laboratories had been conducting research on the human aura, personality survival, and the kinetic powers of the human mind. Most of this research was not made public at the time because of the reluctance with which many scientists view the validation of the mystical traditions. But in recent years increasing numbers of highly respected scientists are coming forward to express their conviction that many of the claims of the mystical traditions can be validated by hard scientific facts. The researchers at the PEAR lab are among the front-runners who are valiantly stepping forward to present some of these facts. But they are not alone. Among the major scientists who believe that science can prove what mysticism and religion have taught for centuries are Paul Davies, a world-famous physicist who is professor of mathematical physics at the University of Adelaide in Australia, and Frank Tipler, a major theoretician in the field of global general relativity and professor of mathematical physics at Tulane University.

In his stunning book *The Mind of God,* Davies states that "We must reject the idea that a physical system, such as a rock or a cloud or a person, is nothing but a collection of atoms, and recognize instead the existence of many levels of structure.... By viewing complex systems as a hierarchy of organizational levels, the simple view of causality in terms of elementary particles interacting with other particles must be replaced by a more subtle formulation in which higher levels can act downward upon lower levels too." This is valiant indeed, but Davies does not simply make statements like this in his book. He goes on to prove them, and he does not hesitate to take on the very popular and powerful quantum mechanics theory to do it. For it is clear that

Davies is very much in Einstein's corner when it comes to a view of the Universe. If the preceding statement conjures visions of the astral world and its many levels, Davies stuns the reader even more when he says that he believes the Universe "looks as if it is unfolding according to some plan or blueprint." Then he hammers this point further by adding that "the essential feature is that something of value emerges as the result of processing according to some ingenious pre-existing set of rules. These rules look as if they are the product of intelligent design. I do not see how that can be denied." These are powerful statements coming from a brilliant and highly respected scientist, and careful as he is to assert his belief in scientific principles, it is transparently clear that he also believes in a designer God. If there is any doubt as to that belief, he quickly disperses it with this parting shot at the end of the book: "I cannot believe that our existence in this universe is a mere quirk of fate, an accident of history, an incidental blip in the great cosmic drama. Our involvement is too intimate. . . . We are truly meant to be here."

If Paul Davies gave validity to the concept of an astral world and its many levels and the existence of a Creator, Frank Tipler takes on reincarnation, the immortality of the soul, and the existence of God in his bestselling book *The Physics of Immortality* An acknowledged atheist, Tipler gave "little thought" to questions of theology, but while devising a mathematical model for the end of the Universe, and "using the most sophisticated methods of modern physics," he realized he had created proof of the existence of God. Tipler called this model the Omega Point Theory. Not only does this theory provide evidence of God's existence, it also proves that it is not only possible, but likely, that every human being who ever lived will be resurrected at the end of the Universe. Tipler uses the Many Worlds Interpretation in the presentation of his theory. This interpretation hints at the possibility of other universes (or astral levels), from the point of view of quantum mechanics. He does this reluctantly, but as he expresses it, "the mathematics forces one to accept it." He also uses quantum cosmology and good doses of classic general relativity to prove his point. He does this with some trepidation but with "quantum" stoicism and determination. At the end of the book, one is left with the feeling that Tipler does not really want to believe in his own theory but is forced by his own evidence to accept it. That is perhaps the most convincing aspect of his book.

This is not to say that most scientists are jumping on the metaphysical bandwagon. In fact, many of them are not, and the ones who are not are openly belligerent about the ones who are.

If physics is the science that shows a more pronounced inclination to flirt with the ideas of a Creator, personality survival, and multiple levels of awareness, biology is the science that stands most adamantly against these same concepts. It is almost as if biologists, deeply enamored of the complexities of matter, believe it capable of accomplishing practically anything, including the creation of the Universe. The branch of biology that stands most resolutely against metaphysical ideas, especially the idea of a soul, is neurobiology. This is the science that endeavors to study and explain the workings of the human brain. Most neurologists grind their teeth at the thought of a human soul. This, they state with assurance, is a hypothesis they have no need of. For it is abundantly clear, they insist, that all the various "supernatural characteristics" ascribed to the soul can be shown to have been produced by the brain.

One of the most recent books to be published based on this assumption was written by Nobel laureate Francis Crick, a world-renowned physicist and biochemist. Some forty years ago, Crick, collaborating with James D. Watson, discovered the molecular structure of DNA, for which they received the Nobel Prize in 1962. His book *The Astonishing Hypothesis* purports that the idea of the soul is a myth and that there is no life before or after this one. Crick considers his hypothesis astonishing because, as he explains it, "Many people are reluctant to accept . . . the reductionist approach that a complex system (like the mind) can be explained by the behavior of its parts and their interconnection with each other." The nature of consciousness itself and the reality of free will are also listed by Crick as reasons why many people reject the idea that our soul is nothing more than a conglomerate of neurons and dendrites interacting with each other. But even though he presents his not-so-astonishing hypothesis with his customary brilliance, Crick is careful to state early in the book that "Not all neuroscientists believe that the idea of the soul is a myth. . . . It is not that they can yet prove the idea to be false," he adds. "Rather, as things stand at the moment, they see no need for that hypothesis."

Sir John Eccles, cited by Crick as one of the neuroscientists who believe in the existence of the soul, and clearly one of the great minds of the twentieth century, said once that the materialistic concept of brain action generating consciousness is patently absurd. He added that any theory of consciousness must deal not only with the brain's effect on the mind but also with the mind's impact on the brain. In his famous book *The Mind and Its Brain*, coauthored with philosopher Sir Karl Popper, Eccles maintains that in addition to brain states determined by physical laws, there are also mental states that fall outside the boundaries of the material world, yet interact with it.

One of the most exciting hypothesis to be recently presented on consciousness was advanced by another neuroscientist, Karl Pribram, head of Radford University's Center for Brain Research and Information Sciences, and by physicist David Bohm, professor emeritus of theoretical physics at Birbeck College in the University of London. In the early stages of his career, Pribram was a confirmed materialist, but he slowly began to realize that the mind had to be more than the results of simple brain activity. He became interested in the science of holography, by means of which three-dimensional images can be created using laser beams. The principle behind the hologram inspired Pribram to conceive the idea that the brain creates three-dimensional versions of the world from electrochemical impulses and then spreads the information across the entire body. Following this idea came the conviction that the Universe also functions as a hologram. Pribram learned by chance of Bohm's studies paralleling his own and immediately seized the opportunity to blend his concept of a holographic mind with Bohm's concept of holographic Universe. In this matter, Pribram was able to formulate a theory of consciousness with deep metaphysical implications where science and mysticism unite as one. Consciousness, he proposed, is an extension of a hidden, larger reality. Mental properties are in reality "the pervasive organizing principles of the universe, which includes the brain."

Erwin Schrödinger, one of the greatest physicists of this century, believed in a collective unconsciousness, or group mind, for all humankind. Schrödinger's famous wave equations form the foundation of quantum mechanics. Openly admitting that he found his inspiration in the study of the

Vedas and the Upanishads, Schrödinger went on to say that "There is obviously one alternative, namely the unification of minds or consciousness. Their multiplicity is only apparent. In truth there is only One Mind."

The famed physicist Sir Arthur Eddington believed that "The idea of a universal Mind or Logos would be a fairly possible inference from the present state of scientific theory; at least it is in harmony with it." One could infer from this statement that science has proven the existence of God.

While scientists battle each other in the awesome task of deciphering the riddles of the Universe, one cannot help but be impressed by their constant fascination with religion and mysticism. It was Fred Hoyle, the creator of the steady-state theory of the Universe, who commented on this fact with subtle irony: "I have always thought it curious that, while most scientists claim to eschew religion, it actually dominates their thoughts more than it does the clergy."

With less flair and considerably more caution, Michio Kaku, a brilliant young professor of theoretical physics at the City College of the City University of New York, presented to the world a vivid exposition of the superstring theory, the new darling of physicists, in his hugely popular book *Hyperspace*. Superstring is to physics what water is to someone dying of thirst. For years physicists have struggled with Einstein's vision of a Unified Theory, where the four major forces of the physical world, gravity, electromagnetism, and the strong and weak nuclear forces are unified harmoniously. This theory, rebaptized as the Theory of Everything, has most scientists scratching their heads, mainly because they cannot seem to be able to unify it. But the superstring concept seems to solve this conundrum with seemingly effortless elegance by envisioning these forces as vibrations in a higher dimensional space. The mathematical snarls created by the Theory of Everything disappear in the superstring world, and their field equations blend together like magic—small wonder physicists love the superstring theory! But what makes it important to this book is the fact that the world of many dimensions evoked by superstring is also strangely similar to the many levels of the astral world. As Kaku explains in his book, superstring theory proposes the existence of ten dimensions. Four of these we are familiar with, the other six are part of yet another "universe" that contracted violently into an almost infinitesimal point at the time of the Big Bang, when our Universe came into being. According to the superstring theory, as Kaku explains in *Hyperspace,* "Before the Big Bang our cosmos was actually a perfect ten-dimensional universe, a world where interdimensional travel was possible. However, this ten-dimensional world was unstable and it "cracked" in two, creating two separate universes: a four and a six-dimensional universe. . . . Our four-dimensional world expanded explosively, while our twin six-dimensional universe contracted violently, until it shrank to infinitesimal size. . . . This theory predicts that our universe has a dwarf twin, a companion universe that has curled up into a six-dimensional ball too small to be observed. This six-dimensional universe . . . may ultimately be our salvation." What Kaku refers to here is the awesome concept presented by late Columbia University physicist Gerald Feinberg, who imagined that in the final moments of the expected collapse of our Universe, our sister Universe would expand once more to allow us to escape destruction through interdimensional travel. And while at this time the superstring theory speaks only of the combined ten dimensions of the two sister universes, there are increasing numbers of scientists who are postulating eleven dimensions instead of ten. That would presuppose that our twin Universe is composed of seven dimensions, which would tend to match the seven levels of the astral world. But whether this twin Universe is composed of six or seven dimensions is of no importance. What seems significant is that the superstring theory gives us a concept of other dimensions different than our own and most importantly the reasons why we cannot see them. They are compressed into a point in space so small as to be invisible to our physical eyes, and inaccessible to our physical bodies, but maybe quite accessible to our equally invisible souls.

So far we have seen how science reluctantly begins to blend with mysticism to embrace the concepts of multiple dimensions easily identifiable with the astral world, the immortality of the soul, the idea of reincarnation, and the concept of a Cosmic Creator or God. What we need now is sufficient faith to live up to all our truly magnificent expectations.

§

preamble

THE SECOND PART OF THIS book is more subjective than the first and deals with the various incarnations of a spirit who calls himself Kirkudian. When I first conceived of the idea for the second part of the book, Kirkudian was not unknown to me. I knew him to be a highly evolved entity, or Aeon, who had lived several of his existences on Earth and had chosen an earthly name to identify his spiritual essence. I chose Kirkudian as the central character of my story as I might have chosen any other spiritual entity. It was basically a whimsical decision because I simply wanted to illustrate a point, to present the concept of reincarnation in a highly personalized way. But I know now that I did not choose Kirkudian as my main character, but rather Kirkudian chose me as a means to tell his story. I know this is not easy to believe. But before you start thinking of me as a fabricator of tall tales, I wish to present you with some facts that support my claim.

The idea of Kirkudian's story and his various incarnations on Earth and in other worlds came to me in several parts, quite slowly, as if the story were unfolding in front of my mind's eye very much as it eventually unfolded in the book. I did not know in the first chapter what was going to happen in the second, and when I wrote the second, I had no idea what was going to happen in the third, the fourth, or any other of the following chapters. This is not the way a writer prepares for a book. There are always countless summaries, story delineations, and several heavily edited drafts before a book is finally put on paper. Of course, the unconscious plays an important part in all of these proceedings, providing the writer with new insights, viable solutions, and the overall quality of the work. But Kirkudian's story refused to be written this way. No matter how hard I tried, my mind drew a blank when I tried to think of what was going to happen in the latter chapters. I finally relented and let the book write itself. There was only one draft—no rewriting was necessary.

Everyone has heard about "character possession" in works of fiction. This happens when one or more of the characters "takes over" and suddenly the writer finds he or she is writing scenes and dialogues for that character that were not part of the original plan for the book. In describing the writing of Kirkudian's story, one could say it was character possession with a vengeance because Kirkudian literally wrote the story. I just sat at the computer and went through the physical motions of putting the story into words.

Some fascinating parts of Kirkudian's story are the historical personages that populate its pages. I was careful to verify some of the historical aspects of those famous lives, but some details appeared to be in direct contradiction with historical data, and those I felt compelled to write as they came to my mind, not as they appear in the history books.

But perhaps the most extraordinary example of the realistic quality of Kirkudian's narrative is his description in chapter 2 of a three-sun solar system he calls Ixistar that, according to him, lies just beyond the Pleiades. Kirkudian describes Ixistar as a solar system composed of fourteen planets, each of which revolves in a triple orbit around the three suns. According to Kirkudian's explanation, each of the planets revolves once around each sun, and when it reaches the aphelion, which is the farthest point away from that sun, it breaks away and falls into the orbit of the next sun, continuing in this manner until it has orbited all three suns, repeating the cycle in a continuous motion. The three suns are equidistant from each other, forming a triangle in space, and all of the fourteen planets revolve around them in triple orbits. Kirkudian calls this solar system one of the most spectacular in that galaxy.

All of this sounds very much like science fiction, but in the October 1995 issue of *Scientific American,* the cover of the magazine depicted an artist's rendition of "three suns and their planets orbiting in a complex gravitational dance." The cover story declares: "The surprising finding that even the youngest stars commonly exist in sets of two or three has revised thinking about the birth of star systems." The author, Alan P. Boss, goes on to imagine the stunning spectacle of a binary system, where the sky would have two suns during the daytime, and sunrises and sunsets would paint the firmament in flaming hues. The two suns might also at times appear to merge, eclipsing each other briefly. If to this fantastic concept is added a third sun, we can well understand why Kirkudian calls Ixistar one of the most spectacular solar systems of its galaxy.

What makes all of this doubly interesting is that this book and Kirkudian's story were written originally in Spanish in 1990 and not published until 1993, two years before the *Scientific American* story appeared on the news-stands. One cannot help but think how fascinating it would be if astrophysicists were to discover Ixistar and endeavor to determine whether the "complex gravitational dance" described by Kirkudian lies within the realm of scientific probabilities.

There is not a great deal more I can tell you about the second part of this book, except that it is very different from anything you may have read about reincarnation and that it will give you food for thought for a long time to come. I hope you enjoy reading Kirkudian's story as much as I enjoyed writing it.

after death

what happens

what happens

after death

part two: kirkudian

after death

what happens

kirkudian

what happens

after death

1 I AM KIRKUDIAN. THAT IS MY
astral name, the name with which I am identified
in the spiritual hierarchy. In reality a soul does
not need a name. Its very essence is enough to
identify it. But names are necessary in the physical realms of being where matter is too dense and
does not allow souls to merge and thus to recognize each other.

Throughout the various worlds I have inhabited and in my many existences, I have had many
names. But now my cycle of incarnations has
ended. My spirit has completed its obligatory sojourn on the material plane. My pilgrimage is over.

A soul's pilgrimage represents the sum of incarnations through which that soul must journey
for its purification. When this forced exile ends,
the soul is offered a choice. It may remain in
whatever level of the astral plane its evolutionary
work has prepared it for, or it may return to the
material world of its choice as either a guide or
protector of one of its inhabitants. In certain
cases, the soul may choose to become the guide
to the collective soul of a race. It may do so as
valor, love, peace, faith, hope, compassion, or
any of the many virtues that help material
beings overcome their baser instincts.

At the end of my pilgrimage, I was offered the
opportunity to be the messenger of sorrow for
humanity. This is an exalted mission because the
experience of sorrow gives a material being the

opportunity to achieve a high degree of purification. If the soul who brings the sorrow accomplishes its task well, the recipient of this experience also receives the healing balm of resignation. By accepting sorrow with resignation, a material being advances in its evolutionary path and ascends toward the divine light. It is a great honor to be offered this mission, but I have never been able to accept sorrow easily. This was one of the hardest lessons I had to learn. Perhaps that is why I suffered so much. But I get ahead of my story.

When I was offered the mission of sorrow, I rejected it. A soul may always choose to accept or reject a mission when offered by its guides, as this is part of its free will. I felt I lacked the spiritual strength to carry it through with any degree of efficacy. But when I was offered the opportunity to become the source of inspiration to an entire race, I was filled with joy. I felt this was a mission I could accomplish successfully. And I quickly accepted the challenge.

I remember my first case clearly. It took place on the third planet of the star called Solaris. Its inhabitants call it Terra, a name that refers to the material from which it is composed. The soul I was called on to help was a young girl from a large section of this planet called, at the time, Imperial Russia. Her name was Anna.

Anna was always a fragile creature, sickly and possessed of a delicate nature that those around her misunderstood or ignored. Yet she had been chosen to serve as an example to the rest of humanity and to become a source of great joy. I came to her side when she was barely nine years old. I remember the great snows that would blanket St. Petersburg every winter and how the river Neva would freeze over before the leaves had begun falling from the trees. I watched along with Anna as the snowflakes fell like angel tears from the leaden skies to the crowded streets below, noisily filled with horses and harried people. The translucent purity of the snow turned ashen quickly under the boots of the pedestrians and the carriage wheels. Hussars of the imperial court often passed under our window, resplendent in their colorful red cassocks, gaudily ornamented with brass buttons and ashtrakan and bearskin furs. Atop their cocky heads sat fur busbies, crowned with regimental plumage.

Anna's large, sad eyes would follow the hussar's arrogant figure as he rode down the street, and to distract her, I would blow gently on her hair or the ribbons of her blouse. She would shake her head or adjust the ribbons, and when she looked again, the rider would have already disappeared around the corner.

No one ever paid much attention to Anna. I was her sole companion on that airy perch two floors above the street. Naturally Anna could not see me. As her spiritual guide, I could not allow her to perceive me. It was imperative to my mission with Anna that she should always believe that the suggestions I whispered in her ear were her own spontaneous thoughts. At no time was she to suspect that those thoughts were emanating from an intelligence alien to her own. It was also necessary that she should be free to choose whether or not to accept the suggestions I implanted in her mind. This was important because my work had to conform at all times with the divine law mandating the free will of all material beings.

When Anna was ten years old, she became gravely ill. Her lungs had always been delicate, and the last two winters had severely affected them. Acute bronchitis became chronic and then turned into double pneumonia, almost destroying her fragile little body. I never abandoned her. Even after her physicians gave up hope on her recovery and her mother's weeping had subsided into exhaustion, I remained by her side, whispering thoughts of spring and its sweet blossoms into her ears. I told her many fairy tales that she repeated in her delirium, and I reminded her many times that she had the strength to overcome her illness and that it was necessary for her to get well because she had something very important to do.

Finally, several months after she was first taken ill, Anna sat up on her bed and asked for food. Her mother, who dozed by her side, nearly fell off her armchair. The doctors had told her that Anna had barely hours left to live. The place became a madhouse. The mother demanded borscht for her daughter at the top of her lungs while the grandmother insisted it was better to give the child mashed potatoes with applesauce. The mother won the battle, and Anna ate two deep bowls of borscht, heaping with sour cream.

After this crisis, the family surrounded Anna with infinite care and tenderness. Her every wish was a command that was promptly obeyed. I whispered to Anna that she should ask her mother to grant her one request. This request was to be enrolled in the Imperial Ballet School. Classical ballet is your destiny, I told her. You shall be a glorious dancer, beloved by all. Emperors and kings will lay their realms at your feet, but your sole desire will be to bring the magic of the dance to the entire world. With winged feet you shall glide across the planet, awakening the loftiest feelings in all who see you. Malice, hatred, jealous rage, and all evil illusions shall lie vanquished at your feet. You alone, by virtue of your art, shall bring an infinite array of human souls to the throne of God.

Her mother could not deny the request of her daughter, barely returned from the doors of death. A few months later, through the intercession of friends of Anna's family, with connections among the Romanoffs, Anna began her studies with the Imperial Ballet School. She was barely eleven.

During the next eight years, I stayed constantly by Anna's side, inspiring her and strengthening her will against all the obstacles she had to face during this period. The competition was fierce, and when Anna made her debut in Russia at the age of eighteen, it went almost unnoticed. But still, I would not allow her to become disheartened. I remained day and night by her side, my words strengthening her will to triumph, my presence fanning the fire of her ambition. At last, Anna was invited on an artistic tour of Scandinavia. The first night she danced outside Russia, she was crowned with glory. From Scandinavia, she went to England and from there to the rest of Europe and the Americas. The echo of her name resounded throughout the world. Her ethereal art, the sublime delicacy of each movement elevated entire audiences to divine regions inhabited by angels and spirits of light. That brief journey increased each soul's vibration, bringing it to higher spheres where all ignoble sentiments were transformed into bliss. During those fleeting moments, each soul perceived the light of the Immortals and longed to remain on those luminous spheres. Upon returning to Earth, some echoes of the experience persisted and helped many souls to rise above their human miseries. That was the end of my mission with Anna Pavlova.

֍

after death

what happens

the first lesson

what happens

after death

2 JUST BEYOND THE PLEIADES
there is a planetary system with three suns called
Ixistar. It has fourteen planets, each of which
moves in a triple orbit around the three suns. It is
a stunning sight when seen from the very center
of Ixistar. Each of the planets completes an orbit
around a sun, and when it reaches the aphelion,
the farthest point from the sun, it breaks away
from the orbit and begins a new one around the
next sun. When it reaches its next aphelion, it
again breaks away to the third sun before returning to its original orbit. The three suns are equidistant, forming a celestial triangle, each point of
which shares the fourteen orbiting planets. None
of the planets moves in the same manner, but
they all travel from sun to sun and from orbit to
orbit. Ixistar is one of the most spectacular solar
systems that exists in that galaxy.

The first planet that journeys around these
three suns is called Firzah. It is a small planet,
and it is very beautiful. Its surface is made of copper crisscrossed with wide veins of aluminum. It
is rich in mineral ores, and in its gleaming
crevasses, one can find deposits of emeralds and
diamonds. Because of its proximity to the three
suns, its atmosphere is too hot to support flora or
fauna of any kind. The beings that inhabit the
planet are formed mostly of gases or minerals. It
was in Firzah that my soul had its first experience
with the material world.

All new souls are innocent. They arrive on the material plane with no concept of what life and living is all about. Their mission is to learn the lessons of the material world, to exist in matter, striving always to purify it without allowing themselves to be contaminated by its powerful emanations. This is not an easy task, and very few souls are able to accomplish their missions in their first incarnations. The material world is dense, and its vibrations can be overwhelming. Most incarnated souls are strongly influenced by matter and wind up losing contact with the higher realms to which they really belong. This is often inevitable because all souls must go through the physical experience, which in turn obliterates the astral echoes, making it difficult for the young soul to remember its mission and its true origin.

At the end of each material existence, the soul has learned new lessons. If it has allowed itself to be overpowered by the material world and in consequence has broken the cosmic laws, it must repeat the same experience repeatedly until it has learned its lessons without breaking the laws.

The first lesson all souls must learn is pain. The soul is immune to pain because it is perfect. Pain is an expression of the imperfection of the material world. The soul knows this, but the body does not. It may suspect the truth, but the power of matter and the apparent evidence of the senses fill it with confusion. The body believes only what it sees—what it perceives to be reality—which is why it suffers pain, whether moral or physical.

I entered into pain early in my physical existence. In my first existence on the planet Firzah, I belonged to the most subtle of life forms on the planet, the gaseous. My body, if you could call it that, was composed of hydrogen, phosphorus, and neon. My form was mobile and changed constantly, giving me the appearance of a phosphorescent golden cloud with silver streaks at its core. Other entities had similar compositions to mine, but there were infinite variations. The more complex the intelligence of the being, the greater the variety of colors it exhibited. Our three regents emitted an indescribable array of colors, like rainbows of iridescent hues.

Life in Firzah is not born. It is created spontaneously, with awareness and understanding, ready to participate in the society to which it belongs. My soul was suddenly enveloped in the vortex of three gases, and my conscience was imprisoned within its nucleus.

My first sensation was one of great anguish, because I did not know who or where I was. Then I was quickly approached by a similar being, who explained the transformation I was undergoing. The communication between that other being and myself was physical but very tenuous. One of his atoms barely interacted with mine, and yet the message I received was complete and instantaneous.

My second sensation was one of great physical pain, an excruciating pain, overpowering and asphyxiating. My very essence writhed in agony in the clutches of that terrible paroxysm. Once again I felt the presence of my companion. His subtle contact revealed to me that the pain was caused by the pressure of the gases within my nucleus. Eventually I would learn to assimilate the pain, he added. But he was mistaken. During the three hundred years I inhabited that vaporous form, I never once felt relief from that terrible pain, and I never assimilated it. Neither was I consoled by the fact that other members of my species suffered from the same annihilating torment. My only consolation on Firzah was Verdigris.

My work on Firzah began the very same moment I attained physical consciousness. The work consisted of exacerbating the activities of the second form of life on the planet, a life that was solid, made up of rocks, metals, and other similar substances. These forms of life interacted with each other, were mobile, reproduced sexually, and were able to expand and grow. They could move across the face of the planet with dizzying speed. Despite their solid forms, they were incredibly light. These mineral beings of Firzah were exquisitely beautiful but possessed of an intelligence inferior to our own. Yet, in spite of our superior intellects, our survival was completely dependent on these life forms because their constant motion produced the gases that gave us life.

Many times I asked myself why my race would desire life if it was to be spent under the constant torment of paralyzing pain. This question was always answered in the same way: Pain is simply a manifestation of the physical body. In reality, it does not exist. And once again my spirit was urged to overcome my misery, to ignore the pain and rise above it. But I never could. My soul was too young and had yet to learn to control my physical reactions.

Part of my duties on Firzah, as it was for others of my race, was to travel across the planet in order to incite the mineral forms to move, expand, and reproduce. This was accomplished by exerting pressure over the surface of the planet where these beings lived.

On the north of Firzah, the surface was made up almost exclusively of beautiful, iridescent rocks in exquisite formations. The perception of beauty confused my spirit because our species did not know how to express admiration or understand desire. Despite this, something within me felt desperately attracted to this place, and I longed to feel physical contact with these beings.

I frequently returned to this place where the rocky formations changed constantly, each one more beautiful than the next. On one of these occasions, I descended rapidly to the surface, which until now I had only observed from above. My vaporous body extended itself like a golden cloud over the most beautiful of the stones, and I caressed it softly. The sensation was immediate and inexplicable. My body trembled spasmodically, and I seemed to lose temporary awareness of myself. This was to me an unknown sensation. The constant pain I suffered disappeared in that instant, and in terror I pulled away from the stone. The pain returned immediately with renewed fury, as if the separation had given it new impetus.

The stone I had touched stirred tremulously, and its luminous colors glowed and deepened. From within those pulsating hues arose a green and silver cloud that floated slowly toward me. It was a new form of life, created through me, born from my ephemeral contact with the stone. This was how Verdigris came into my life.

From that moment on, nothing was ever to be the same. During my existence on Firzah, my contacts with other members of my species had always been telepathic. I had never felt emotion or sentiment in our dealings. Ours was an intellectual civilization where emotions were nonexistent. But Verdigris transformed all my perceptions. Through her I became aware of the meaning of my own existence because I shared everything with her, my life and my soul.

When I perceived her essence for the first time, I felt compelled to establish contact immediately, and her touch permeated my soul with joy. Verdigris did not feel the pain that tormented the rest of our race. Her contact was sweet and soft and full of ineffable tenderness. Her soul shone with the same gemlike, crystalline light that radiated from the stone that had given her life. My pain did not vanish with her contact, but it made it more tolerable.

From that instant, Verdigris and I became inseparable. We traveled the far reaches of that planet and worked together to create new life. But we never returned to the place where she had come into being.

Verdigris's presence gave meaning to my existence on Firzah. Our mutual attraction intensified with the passing of time, and periodically, after finishing our work, we would unite our essences in order to multiply our energies. It wasn't a sensuous union; those feelings were unknown to our race. But it was more powerful than a simple physical union. It was the total identification of our souls, the fusion of our identities, of our thoughts, of our very essences.

Verdigris did not really belong to our race. The force that drove my species and kept us constantly active was the ever-present pain that haunted us eternally. Verdigris did not know this pain. Her existence was enveloped in a whirlwind of silver and emerald, a wondrous joy of being, and an intense awareness of all that was beautiful on that planet.

I do not know when I first noticed the weakening of her vital force. I sensed it during one of our unions. Her soul did not vibrate with the same intensity. Her strength began to fade with the same exquisite tenderness that characterized her whole being. Something inside me shuddered with fear. Verdigris felt it, and her happiness abated for a moment. But it was reborn a second later, stronger than ever. Her message arrived in flickers of light. "Do not fear," she said. "We shall find each other again, in other lives, in other worlds."

From that moment on, her essence began to grow fainter until finally it vanished completely. I cannot express how I felt at that moment. I have already said that emotions did not exist for our race. But Verdigris had opened up new possibilities in my life; she had created new sentiments in me and had accelerated the evolution of my spirit. Something in me died when she died. The monstrous pain of my body seemed to recede before the overwhelming pain within my soul. In desperation I returned to the place where one hundred years before I had touched the face of the stone and Verdigris had emerged. The landscape had changed completely. The stones had disappeared. In their place a wide sea of liquid copper stretched in amber waves toward the horizon.

Maddened with grief, I rose to the highest reaches of our atmosphere and dissolved my essence in the midst of space. The various gases that formed my being dissipated quickly in shimmering streaks of gold and silver. The pain that had accompanied me through three centuries of life on Firzah disappeared only with my death.

I do not know if the other members of my race noticed my passing. But I do know they did not mourn me. On that planet, and for that species, those feelings do not exist.

It was not physical pain that I rejected with my self-destruction; it was the pain of my soul. That rejection condemned me to relive the same experience and learn the same lesson through many existences.

If I had known the price I would have to pay because of my impulsive action, I would have tried to live with my sorrow. I am not a coward. I suffered during three long centuries the most destructive physical pain that can possibly be imagined. If I destroyed my life, if I refused to continue my existence, it was not out of cowardice but out of love. After having shared my existence with Verdigris, I could not conceive living it without her.

Poor deluded fool! How bitterly I was to pay for my actions. How much pain I would have to endure, how many lives I would have to live, how many centuries would have to pass before I could again meet with Verdigris.

§

after death

what happens

**soul
mates**

what happens

after death

3 ALL SOULS ARE REQUIRED TO undergo many lives or incarnations in their quest for spiritual purification. This does not mean that they share the same number of experiences, or for that matter, an equal amount of time in the material plane. Certain souls may require more time and incarnations than others in order to complete their cycle of learning. Failure to learn any one lesson may require the soul to relive similar existences many times until that particular lesson has been completely assimilated.

As I said before, the hardest lesson I had to learn was that of sorrow. During countless centuries, I was forced to inhabit different bodies and face many harrowing and soul-shattering experiences in my futile efforts to escape the unavoidable. I just could not accept the experience.

The desperation that drove me to terminate my existence in Firzah cost me dearly. At the end of that life, I fell into what can only be described as a profound sleep, after which I awoke feeling strong and full of renewed energy. At that moment I did not know how long I had slept, nor had I any knowledge of the place where I awoke. Later I learned that I had been asleep for two thousand Terra years and that the place where I then found myself was the vestibule of souls on the Second Astral Plane.

The first thing I noticed upon awakening was that I was floating horizontally in an immense open space. My physical form was the same I had on Firzah. Facing me I saw two unknown entities, both of whom were surrounded by a cloud of resplendent light. In silent words that echoed in my mind, they told me that they were my guides, souls who had been chosen by a Supreme Intelligence to help me adapt to my new state. The questions that burned like seeds of fire in my mind were answered before I expressed them. In this telepathic form, I was told that my rejection of life on Firzah had not been recorded in my Trianic Record because the reason for my rash action had been love for another being, and love is the highest of cosmic emanations. But they went on to explain that the lesson I had rejected was still to be learned.

The Trianic Record, they explained, is a list of the violations of any of the three major Cosmic Laws by a soul, whether free or incarnated. These three laws are simple. The first says that a soul should never function or act as One, but as part of the All. The second says that a soul should never forfeit its evolutionary advancement through the avoidance of experience. And the third says that a vessel of experience—such as a physical form—should never be willfully destroyed. These three laws have three important codicils that are not laws in themselves but seeds of enlightenment that lead to the return to the Force, which is the ultimate aim of evolution. The first codicil says that self-sacrifice for the sake of another is a sign of approaching enlightenment, for the soul recognizes at that point in its evolution that all others are parts of itself. The second codicil says that acceptance in all its forms is the seed of humility—the most precious of all virtues—and leads to bliss. The third codicil says that love leads to regeneration and total union and is the source of the All.

The three laws and the three codicils are encoded within a soul as it is emanated from the All, but it often forgets them when it is imprisoned in a physical form, pursuing its path of evolution. The All—that is, the Creator or Cosmic Oversoul—manifests its essence in the form of myriad souls for the purpose of experiencing matter. Each soul is a part of it, and to it must each soul eventually return, each cycle of experiences completed and the soul purified through the path of evolution.

I wanted to know why I still retained my original form when I remembered having destroyed it in Firzah. My guides, who I learned to differentiate as Jeremiah and Joab, explained that the reason I still saw my body as it had existed in Firzah was because that was the way I conceived myself. The physical pain I had endured during so many centuries had disappeared because that was part of the experience I had to undergo in that existence.

When I asked about Verdigris, the dazzling light that surrounded the figures flickered softly. They told me that in the natural order of the Universe, everything has a dual nature, positive and negative, masculine and feminine. From the heart of the atom, proton, and electron to the most advanced beings, all that exists is formed of opposite charges in perfectly harmonious balance. From this perfect union arose light and life. Twin souls, or soul mates, united in love—like the atom, like God—are hermaphroditic in essence because their combined entity encompasses both the male and the female. Therefore, in their natural state, two souls—positive and negative energies, male and female in the physical worlds—exist as one essence. But when this dual energy vortex that is the soul manifests in the physical world, it is temporarily divided into two halves so that it may experience each individual trait and recognize the importance of union. It often happens that the female aspect of the soul is incarnated into a male physical body—and vice versa—which creates pain and confusion for the soul that knows its true gender. Only after a series of incarnations, during which each half of the soul immerses itself in the material world, transcends it, and purifies itself, can the two halves meet again and reunite for eternity.

But the material world is powerful, and eventually each half of the incarnated soul becomes wrapped up in its new body and life and forgets its true spiritual essence. Often this causes it to fail in the assimilation of the experiences of a lifetime.

The one thing a soul never forgets is that it is incomplete, that an intrinsic part of its essence is missing. That is why as long as it is incarnated in a physical body, the soul searches constantly and unconsciously for its missing half and is often attracted to those beings who remind it, however faintly, of its true soul mate or twin soul. This search is generally in vain, as it is very rare for twin souls to be incarnated in the same place at the same time. When this happens, however, the attraction is immediate and all-encompassing, even though the two soul mates may not know the reason for its intensity. But for the most part, only one soul incarnates at a time, while the other remains in the astral plane.

Verdigris, according to Joab and Jeremiah, was my twin soul, the other half of my spirit. When I touched the stone in Firzah, the other half of my soul, who was Verdigris, felt the irresistible urge to incarnate and be by my side. By doing this she broke the First Cosmic Law because we were not to meet for several incarnations. Therefore she acted not for the sake of the All but for the sake of the One, our united being. Because of this and because I had left my life prematurely, we would have to be separated for a long time until the Cosmic Laws we each had broken were reestablished.

As soon as I understood this, I was overwhelmed with anguish. How, I asked, can I shorten the time I am to be separated from Verdigris? The answer came to me in a sudden flash, before I had finished asking the question: through acceptance and obedience.

A new existence was then offered to me through which I would be able to make considerable progress in my spiritual evolution. The new lessons awaiting me were once again the control of my emotions, especially sorrow and pain.

Filled with exaltation, I quickly accepted this new life, eager to undergo any test, however severe, that would hasten the moment of my reunion with Verdigris. But my guides viewed my excitement with less enthusiasm. "You are still a very young soul," they cautioned. "Control your impetuosity. This next life will be very difficult, and it will have many temptations. You must not give in to them." But I was hardly listening. My soul only longed to reincarnate as swiftly as possible so that I might advance with giant steps toward the precious moment when I would once again be together with Verdigris.

My next existence took place in a planetary system known as Varnya. This group of planets orbited a bright red star by the same name, which was nearing the stage at which it would become a supernova. When this happens, the star explodes violently, and its massive energy is absorbed within itself, creating a powerful vortex of such indescribable power that it rends the very fabric of space, opening a hole that leads into other Universes. These Universes are separate levels of existence, which are part of the astral world. There are millions of these holes across the Universe and they all lead to different astral planes.

The planet into which I was to enter my second existence was the seventh from Varnya and was called Del.

Despite its great distance from the dying star, the red light emitted by Varnya was so powerful that it bathed Del in its rays day and night. The atmosphere of the planet was also a brilliant scarlet that colored everything on its surface with fiery hues. Del's surface was composed of iron, molybdenum, and a third element, tritium, whose bright red color gives Del its bloodlike atmosphere. Tritium has a nucleus considerably heavier than uranium but far more stable.

The entire surface of Del is crisscrossed by rivers of liquid tritium. Red vegetation grows thickly everywhere, with deep, immense roots that twist their way underground to the rivers' edges to take nourishment from the flaming liquid. Life is short on Del. In contrast with my long existence on Firzah, I lived on the scarlet planet barely ten years. They were years filled with amazing experiences.

There exists on Del an infinity of organisms: liquid, solid, gaseous, as well as two species that belong to their own special class. The first of these, called Silomi, has the appearance of a viscous, gelatinous form, but in reality it has no substance. Neither liquid nor solid, it can best be described as amorphous. The second unique form of life, called Yartha, has the appearance of a nebulous gas, but in reality it is quite solid. Its contact is deadly. Yartha may be compared to a predatory animal. The Silomi is its avowed enemy, and they war constantly.

In this, my second existence, I formed part of the flora of the planet. My body was that of a leafy tree whose trunk was made up of elements that gave it a purple hue interspersed with orange veins. My foliage was also orange, and twice during my existence I blossomed with purple fruit. My mission was to maintain my being in inner harmony and to make sure that the interaction of the species around me also took place in harmony. My branches were my children, and my leaves, our protection. Every day I would extend my roots through the surface to seek the molten rivers that nourished me. My life would have passed uneventfully if it hadn't been for the other species who shared the planet with me.

The animal species of Del, called Yartha, was indescribably malevolent. It destroyed everything it came in contact with for no special reason, except its enjoyment of inflicting pain. It was the most intelligent being on Del and the most powerful. In contrast to the other species who inhabited the scarlet planet and flourished in abundant varieties, Yartha was an entire species within itself; it was one sole being. This unique creature was inexpressibly beautiful and equally ferocious. It was androgynous, and although it was not a sexual entity in the terrestrial sense of the word, it encompassed a duality in its essence that can be described only as both male and female in unison. Its body was a gleaming emerald surface of perfectly symmetrical proportions that changed constantly, each varying form exhibiting such exquisite harmony as to be a delight to the senses. Only the knowledge of its cruelty and cunning kept the other species of Del away from this resplendent being, for Yartha's touch meant sudden and terrible death to whichever unfortunate creature might cross its path. Anything it touched was absorbed by Yartha at a slow and asphyxiating pace. It seemed to relish the agony of its victims by prolonging their death throes with venomous cunning. Thus Yartha fed, vastly unchallenged, on all the other life forms on Del. Its appetite was voracious and its destructive instincts unparalleled in their malignity. During its frequent hunting forays, it would leave nothing alive in its wake.

The only species on Del that could successfully stand up to Yartha was Silomi, a gelatinous creature that was as physically repulsive as its soul was compassionate and generous.

The floral species of Del to which I belonged had the ability to move from place to place if they so desired. With hypersensitive roots, I could feel the path that Yartha was taking and was able to protect myself and my children by moving away when I felt Yartha approaching.

The first time my branches blossomed and gave fruit, Yartha was scavenging on the other side of the planet; when it finally made its way to us, all of my fruit had been consumed by the other creatures in our immediate surroundings. Yartha's rage knew no bounds when it discovered all the fruit had been eaten, as they were the rarest and most exquisite on Del. Each tree of my species blossomed and gave fruit only twice during its lifetime, making its fruit doubly desirable.

Many thousands of creatures perished that day because of Yartha's fury. When its rage had abated somewhat, it swore that when I bore fruit once more, it would be the only one to consume them. Yartha made another promise at this time, swearing to destroy me when it had consumed my next bounty. What good would I be after this, it snarled, since I would not be bearing fruit again?

As the years passed, I continued to avoid Yartha. Silomi had become my ally, promising to defend me against the destructive venom of our common enemy. And one beautiful morning, as the russet tones of our sun spread over the horizon, my branches brought forth their fruit for the last time. The branches, my children, filled with joy at the splendid sight. This time my fruit was bigger and more succulent than during the first harvest. All the many species of the planet surrounded us, asking to share in our bounty. My branches shook joyfully, spreading the amethyst-hued fruit all around us.

Suddenly I saw Silomi rise before me. Its urgent message reached me through the tenuous whistle it used to communicate. In this manner it told me that Yartha was approaching quickly and that I must move away as fast as possible. Being laden with heavy fruit made movement difficult for me, and before I was able to communicate this to Silomi, Yartha's grandiose structure towered over us. Never had the creature seemed more beautiful. Its lithe yet supple body shone with iridescent hues, and the perfection of its form was only enhanced by the grace of each movement. For a fleeting moment, I stared at it, unable to move, entranced by its majestic beauty. By the time I had regained the power to move, Yartha was already upon me, viciously tearing at my branches and my trunk.

Silomi came between us bravely, but this time Yartha's strength was multiplied by the hate and destructive wrath that propelled it. Again and again, Silomi attacked Yartha, only to be repulsed each time by the fiend's awesome power. In between each bout with Silomi, Yartha continued to lunge at my trunk, shredding and tearing at my branches. The latter were the most dear to me and were also the weakest part of my being. They relied on me for strength and sustenance, but I was unable to help them now. Each time Yartha attacked one of my branches, it destroyed it forever.

Filled with desperation, both a victim and a witness to this terrible massacre, I was unable to flee because by now Yartha had completely attached itself to my trunk. I knew my death was imminent just as I knew that I should accept it and surrender my essence to the cosmos. But something within me rebelled against meek surrender. Trembling with pain and hopeless rage, I forced my roots out of the iron ground in which they lay embedded and frantically wrapped them like coils about Yartha's body. The creature's strength was terrifying, but desperation gave me the edge in the struggle. Tangled in this way with my enemy, driven by my pain, I dragged myself to the scarlet river that had for so long nourished me and threw myself and my vile cargo into its turbulent currents. Within moments, we both sank into the ruby depths forever.

This time I slept for a thousand Terra years. When I awoke, I once again found myself in the vestibule of souls. My two guides were by my side. I was floating once again, suspended in midair, but this time my essence was composed of a single reddish point of light. At the initial moment of consciousness, the memories of my two previous existences and all the experiences I had during them came rushing to me in a dizzying flow of images. I relived both existences completely in those moments but without emotion, as if I were watching the scenes of a drama unfold before me and I were a mere spectator. The only thing that made my spirit shudder was the memory of Verdigris.

"You cannot as yet find each other." The unspoken message came to me from Jeremiah as soon as he perceived my thoughts.

"Why not?" I asked.

"Because you have passed through two existences to learn the lesson of sorrow but continue to reject it," he answered in silence. "Only when you have assimilated and understood this experience can you unite again with Verdigris."

These words filled me with despair. "But what has been my offense?" I cried. "All I did was defend myself against a monster. Is it just for one being to destroy another with impunity? What is the purpose of such a lesson?"

Joab answered this time, and his message was filled with a gentle sadness.

"The purpose of the lesson is to teach you that pain and sorrow are illusions of the physical world. They exist only in the context of matter. If you had accepted your sorrow on Del with humility and surrendered your soul to the Creator, you would have assimilated the lesson and advanced greatly in your evolution and your quest for your twin soul. And Yartha, far from being a monster, is a highly evolved entity who has chosen as its exalted mission to impart the important lesson of sorrow to an entire planet."

My astonishment was so great at these words that for a moment I was too stunned to answer. But suddenly all the memories of Yartha's cruelty and vicious cunning came rushing to my soul, filling me with outrage and revulsion.

"How can this be so?" I cried. "How can such vile and cruel actions be the mark of an evolved being? If that is so, I do not look forward to spiritual evolution."

The rebellious words had no sooner left my mind than I was filled with great remorse.

"Forgive me," I said humbly. "I did not mean those harsh words. But I am utterly filled with confusion. I know your kindness and concern for my soul. Please enlighten me. Do not abandon me now."

"How can we abandon you when you are a part of us?"said Jeremiah gently. "Your confusion is natural. There is much for you to learn still."

The second guide, Joab, extended his shimmering light like a brilliant robe over my troubled soul. I was instantly at peace, and a great joy permeated my being.

"Do not torment yourself, beloved child; listen. You remember Yartha's cruelty but forget its beauty, such beauty and symmetry of form that it enthralled your senses whenever you beheld it. Do you recall how Yartha encompassed within itself an entire species? That is because it was the collective soul of a race. That only happens when a species is so highly evolved as to merge all the various consciousnesses that make the species into one whole. It is the first step a race must take before becoming One with the Universal Force. Yartha knows well what sorrow is, for it has experienced sorrow individually and collectively in myriad forms and ways. And it knows that sorrow is a mirage, just as pleasure and joy are mirages, and it wanted to impart that knowledge to you and the other beings on Del. Yartha was Del's purificator: its athanor."

I was mystified. "What is an athanor?"

"The means of experiencing a lesson for the soul or undergoing purification when it has broken one of the three Cosmic Laws," said Joab. "Sometimes an advanced spiritual entity undertakes this mission for the benefit of one or more souls. Such was the case with Yartha."

"But what is reality to the soul?" I asked, still confused.

"Peace eternal, perfect harmony, and cosmic union," said Joab gently. "That is ecstasy, a feeling so sublime you cannot comprehend it as yet, but what you can aspire to when you reach the higher states of spiritual evolution."

My soul basked for a long time in the half-envisioned bliss Joab's words conjured in my mind. But then new doubts stirred deep within me.

"But how can I remember such aspirations when I am incarnated again? All my previous memories and your teachings are erased as soon as I am born into matter."

"The body you are born into forgets your past, but your soul does not," said Jeremiah. "If you harmonize yourself with your inner true self, you will know instinctively how to act in each incarnation."

"What will happen now? Will I be punished?" I asked, still filled with misgivings.

"There is no such thing as punishment." This time Jeremiah and Joab answered in unison. "Each existence carries its own lessons and burdens, which the soul must assimilate and accept. When it does not, or whenever it breaks any of the Cosmic Laws, it must be purified through an athanor, which is always a disturbing experience to a soul. You may think of it as punishment, but in reality it is the soul itself who creates its unhappy experiences, like you have done in your past two incarnations. There are many souls in the lower levels of the astral world who continually reject lessons and break the laws and in this way prolong their separation from the Cosmic Light."

"What will happen to me now?"

"There is a new Yartha in Del. And you still have to learn the lesson of sorrow. But not now. In your next incarnations, you will struggle against vanity, pride, avarice, egotism, fear, insecurity, jealousy, doubt, lust for power, untoward ambition, lies, crime, and other illusions of matter. When you have conquered them all, you will once more wrestle with your steadfast enemies: pain and sorrow. All you need to sustain you is hope and trust. Are you ready for your next physical experience?"

These words of Jeremiah were to echo for many a millennia and many a lifetime in my soul, but now they just filled me with joy and anticipation.

"Yes, I am ready!" I cried exultantly. "I am ready for my next pilgrimage."

The two guides rose above me. A white blinding light surged from their united essence and enveloped my spirit. I immediately lost consciousness. When I regained it, I had been incarnated again.

§

after death

what happens

many worlds

what happens

after death

4 JEREMIAH HAD SAID THAT I
still had to face and conquer sorrow but that first
I had to learn other lessons through several lifetimes. The cycle of incarnations varies from soul
to soul and is determined by their ability to learn
and assimilate each lesson.

In my next existence, I inhabited the consciousness of the waters of a planet called Ardanis, which is found just beyond the Pleiades. It
was a long life without complications. Perhaps
Jeremiah and Joab thought an agreeable existence advisable after the tempestuousness of my
first two. My lesson on this planet was patience.
The waters were never in a hurry and had no
pressing concerns, except to flow steadily in the
same direction. Their lives were filled with serenity and acceptance of the Cosmic Laws.

Ardanis was one of three small planets that
revolved around a beautiful and brilliant sun,
whose light refracted over Ardanis in a rainbow
of indescribable colors. All three planets were
inhabited by the same advanced race of extraordinary intelligence, whose main occupation was
the exploration of the galaxies. Over the last million years, they had traveled to the confines of the
Universe.

The three planets, Ardanis, Dramanis, and
Gratilis, had evolved identically and were quite
close to one another. The inhabitants called

themselves Drekogi and accomplished their intergalactic voyages by means of tertiary rays, which transported them instantaneously to whatever planet or system they wished to visit. They were called tertiary rays because they interconnected with the three planets. Their source was the combined mental energy of the Drekogi.

The waters of Ardanis were composed not of hydrogen and oxygen, like the waters of Terra, but of a mixture of mercury and liquid nitrogen. This made the waters of Ardanis viscous yet translucent with silver highlights. The consciousness of the waters ebbed and flowed with its currents; that is to say, it moved from wave to wave, sending its thoughts along the entire breadth of its body. This is how I lived for five hundred years, floating from one extreme of Ardanis to the other, exchanging experiences with the waves and receiving in my essence the incandescent impact of the tertiary rays that illuminated my understanding with their radiant vibrations.

The Drekogi were a race of great cosmic sensibilities, and they tried to elevate the collective intelligence of each race they visited. On the planet Terra, which they visited periodically, they made their presence felt by implanting members of their race among the local populations. These Drekogi were generally implanted as scientists or gifted thinkers who helped to evolve the consciousness of the planet and its inhabitants. At no time were they perceived to be extraterrestrials. In actuality, the inhabitants of Terra were constantly waiting for visits from extraterrestrials without realizing they had been living among them for centuries.

The end of my existence on Ardanis took place as abruptly as it had begun. My conscience simply abandoned the waters and found itself once again face to face with Joab and Jeremiah.

"Five hundred years of peace have greatly helped your spirit," said Jeremiah. "Your aura has acquired more light and the red glow has disappeared."

"Why did you take me away from Ardanis?" I asked. "I was happy there. I would have liked to remain on Ardanis forever."

"Have you so quickly forgotten Verdigris?" Jeremiah responded.

My soul was suddenly flooded by the memories of my past existences and with them the longing for my beloved Verdigris. I felt my life force choking within me.

"Verdigris!" I cried in despair. "What has happened to Verdigris? You promised me we would soon be together. How much longer must I wait for that reunion?"

"You have barely begun your pilgrimage, and yet you already despair of your mission. Five hundred years of peace on Ardanis should have taught you more patience," spoke Joab, his brilliant countenance shimmering in the cosmic light.

"You are right," I said, filled with shame. "I need to assimilate each lesson more thoroughly. Patience has been the most beautiful lesson up till now. I think it will help me face the coming trials with greater spiritual strength."

"Your words fill me with great satisfaction," answered Joab. "They indicate that you have advanced a great deal in your evolutionary path. We have communed with the Great White Council that is in charge of spirits at your astral level, and it has been determined that the remainder of your physical lifetimes will be spent in the planetary system called Solaris. This system is composed of twelve orbiting planets, each of which has its own distinct life forms. They are so distinct indeed that none of them is aware of the others' existence. The planet in closest orbit to Solaris is known universally as Merkur. It is a tiny planet with a molten surface due to its proximity to Solaris. Life exists there in gaseous and liquid states, not unlike those you knew in your first existence on Ixistar. Its spiritual level is in the midrange of the astral light, but its rate of evolution is accelerating rapidly. Soon it will develop an interest in the rest of the manifested universe. In the second orbit, there is a planet called Veneris whose surface is hidden by thick clouds. These are the result of a heavy atmosphere composed of sulphur and titanium. Life on Veneris exists in the gaseous, liquid, and solid states and in an infinite variety. Intelligence varies from species to species, but there is one particular type of gaseous life that communicates telepathically and has no need of a solid form. This is the species that controls Veneris, and they are known as Tepsech."

"Is that how we know them, or is that what they call themselves?" I asked Joab.

"The names of the various races and planets are the same all over the Universe," answered the guide. "They are transmitted telepathically to each race by the forces governing the cosmos."

"What planet follows Veneris?"

"The planet Terra, which is in the third orbit around Solaris. On Terra, life expresses itself in gaseous, liquid, and solid states and also in an infinity of species. Nearly all of them communicate with each other telepathically. The exception is one race of the middle order. They are of the solid state and are known as Humanitas in the cosmos. They call themselves humanity and are convinced they are the most intelligent race on the planet. They are not. The most intelligent species is of the gaseous form and is called Etheris. They have a complex hierarchy and are greatly advanced. It is they who protect the planet and keep other species, like

Humanitas, under control. They also constantly help them; in a way, they may be said to be the older siblings of the human race. The humans themselves are a chosen race and are at the threshold of their spiritual and material evolution. Although they are a noble race, the slow progress of their evolution has put their future in peril. If they can survive the current period without destroying themselves, they have the potential to achieve the greatest level of spiritual and material evolution in their galaxy."

"What is the danger that threatens them?" I asked.

"Their inability to understand and harmonize matter and their belief that the physical world is everything," answered Jeremiah.

"But don't they learn anything during their lives on Terra?" I wondered.

"Naturally," said Jeremiah. "But the planet is very beautiful, and it causes them to develop a powerful desire to remain on Terra forever, enjoying the many pleasures that are possible there."

"I don't understand what you are talking about," I said. "In all my existences, I have never experienced any of these pleasures."

"You are still very young," replied Joab. "You would never have been able to resist the temptations of Terra if we had sent you there first. Souls go there in their final stages of physical evolution. It is a planet where the spirit is severely tempted and tormented. Many cannot resist these influences and break the Cosmic Laws continuously or else refuse to assimilate their appointed lessons. But others pass through the peak of terrestrial experience in so sublime a manner that they end their physical pilgrimage there. But the vast majority learn only part of their lessons and have to repeat the existences over and over again."

"Who tempts these people of Terra?" I asked.

"The Vreckli," answered Jeremiah. "They work with the athanors, whose mission is to test souls in the assimilation of their lessons."

"Was Yartha a Vreckli?" I asked.

"No, Yartha is the oversoul of an entire species belonging to the planet Del. It chose to be the planet's athanor to help accelerate its evolution. The Vreckli work with the athanors of different species and belong to a high cosmic order."

"Have they tempted me at any time?"

"Naturally. You have been tempted in each existence," Joab said. "It is their mission, and it is a vital mission for the evolution of the cosmos."

"Why had you said nothing about the Vreckli before now?" I demanded.

"Because you would not have understood. But now your intellect has evolved enough for you to receive this lesson," said Jeremiah. "If you learn it well, it will help you a great deal in your future existences."

"But how can I recognize the Vreckli?" I insisted, fascinated by the concept of these strange creatures. "What do they look like?"

The brilliant light that emanated from the two guides changed perceptibly. Joab's form became more discernible through the cloud of light covering it. I perceived a being of transcendental beauty who seemed to oscillate in a sea of blinding cosmic radiance.

"The Vreckli do not manifest themselves in light, but rather in darkness," he said. "They are part of the chaos from which surged the first cosmic manifestation. As such they are counted among the Elder Brethren of the First Council. But do not concern yourself thinking about them. Their mission is not destruction, but purification. You could not understand it at your present level. The Vreckli simply complete the task designated for them by the Creative Force of the Universe, of which they are a part even as you and I are."

"Which are the planets that come after Terra?" I asked, realizing that neither of my guides wanted to speak any further on the subject of the Vreckli.

"Marek is in the fourth orbit," said Jeremiah. "Its surface is a great desert of red sands. Its most common elements are carbon, oxygen, and copper, and their combinations have formed solid, rocklike life forms. They are not highly evolved. The manifestation of their cosmic conscience is tenuous, and they develop very slowly. In the fifth orbit there is a gigantic planet named Herschel, whose gaseous atmosphere is mostly made up of hydrogen and helium along with a great many compounds of ammonia. It is unique in the system in that its surface is composed entirely of gaseous layers. In its center these gases are extremely hot and produce great turbulence on its surface."

"Is there life, souls like me, in these places?" I asked.

"There is life of great spiritual evolution," answered Joab. "The surface of Herschel is one of the most important fountains of cosmic energy in that galaxy. Many interplanetary travelers stop there to reenforce their energies, as do many astral beings, in order to establish contact with other cosmic forces. All life on Herschel is gaseous and possessed of tremendous spiritual capacities. Again their advancement is such that it would be difficult for you to grasp it in your present evolutionary state."

"What other planets are there in Solaris?" I prompted.

"After Herschel there is Saternas, a planet with great concentric rings around it. The rings are composed of gases and rocks, and they are in turn controlled by the two small moons that orbit around the planet. It is on these moons that the most advanced intelligence of Saternas has developed; it is a highly evolved species of rock life. After

Saternas come the orbits of Neptunias, Urantis, Pratilis, Vristel, Draconis, and Kreptis. All these planets are inhabited by species of greatly advanced intelligence in distinct manifestations. Kreptis, the last of these planets, is home to a life form of solid liquid, that is to say a type of ice composed of water and argon. The light of Solaris barely reaches this planet. It is encompassed by near total darkness, and its only illumination is the result of a light that is created by the conjunction of certain gases, neon and argon predominating. Its intelligence is vast and its evolution extraordinary. Its influence maintains the harmony of the Solaris system. Eventually, when all the species reach their collective evolutionary zenith, they will join together in a bond that will transform their galaxy and, ultimately, the entire Universe. That is why every planet in this system is important and has its own guides to rule and protect it."

Joab finished speaking, and his light joined with Jeremiah's to form a luminous fountain of dazzling brilliance.

"What have you learned from all this?" they asked in unison.

"That I am very small, very young, and would like to know more," I replied.

"You will be granted that opportunity immediately. This time you will have the chance to learn many lessons and experience many things in one existence."

"What kind of lessons?" I cried excitedly. "Tell me what kind, and where?"

"Terra is the place, and the lessons deal with the pleasures you asked about before. Along with the experience of pleasure, you will have the opportunity to feel avarice, jealousy, and lust, and fall under the destructive influence of power and crime. It will not be an easy existence, and you must remember in the deepest part of your soul that the Vreckli will tempt and torment you during your entire lifetime. If they succeed, you will have to spend many more lives before you can meet with Verdigris."

"And will you be with me?" I asked tremulously, my spirit gripped by a heretofore unknown sensation that I was later to know as fear.

"We will always be by your side. You will never be alone, even if you don't perceive us," said both guides. "May your soul remain strong through the trials that are to come."

The light was extinguished, and I once again lost consciousness. When I awoke, I was on Terra.

§

after death

what happens

terra

what happens

after death

5 My first impression of Terra

was of cold, an icy, biting cold. Rough hands pulled me out of a warm and comfortable place where I had been floating for what seemed like an eternity. I expressed my displeasure immediately in a loud and surprisingly squealy voice. Remembering my promise to my guides, I tried to temper that displeasure with some of the patience I had learned on Ardanis, but it was poor consolation.

The same rough hands proceeded to wash me in a warm liquid and wrapped my body in a coarse fabric. Later I learned that the fabric was actually the finest of linens, but at the moment it felt like the gravel of Del to my sensitive skin. I was fed immediately from a soft and warm fountain, and the sustenance I drew from it was agreeable if somewhat rancid. Later I learned that this fountain was my mother's breast.

The first days of my existence were quite pleasant, alternating between a sweet, deep sleep and shorter periods of cold and great discomfort. When I was awake, I spent my time being passed around into many hands, and although I did not understand the people's language, I could feel that my presence was a source of great pleasure to those around me. If this is the difficult existence that Jeremiah and Joab spoke of, let me remain here forever, I thought to myself with satisfaction.

As time went on, I began to recognize the different people around me, and slowly I started to understand their language. My mother was beautiful, a woman of exquisite features, but with a terrible disposition. She reproached my father daily for his coldness toward her and his many absences. He never answered her, but it was not hard for me to read on his tired face the great effort it took not to argue with her.

The place where I lived those first few months was very pleasant. My bed was bordered in gold and was always in the open air, facing a beautiful turquoise sea. The women who took care of me were Nubian, and their ebony skin contrasted pleasingly with the white linens they always wore.

At first, my mother came to see me twice a day. But after a while, her visits grew rarer, and eventually she only stopped by once or twice a week, and then only briefly. At that time, my meals came from an enormous woman with a child younger than I whom she fed only after I had eaten. Perhaps because there was not enough sustenance for both of us, the other child was pale and thin. His mother never complained about so obvious an injustice, and she continued to come and feed me four times a day. One day she arrived without this other infant, whom I never was to see again. I don't know if the child died or what his or her fate was. In a short while, the woman stopped coming also. My meals were changed to goat's milk, which I found a great deal more appetizing.

I was visited periodically by Joab and Jeremiah, who instructed me telepathically about the mission I was to undertake on Terra. They would no longer be able to come and see me after a while, they told me. The influences of Terra would start to be felt very soon, and I was going to forget the reason for my existence. It was necessary that I instruct my inner self to remember in silence their instructions so that these would not be lost.

Communication between my guides and me did not take place in any language; rather, it was a mental osmosis that traversed our spirits. It was never necessary to externalize our thoughts, as they were perceived by us the instant they were formed. On the other hand, on Terra, each person spoke differently, and it was easy for me to see that many of the things they said were not echoed in their hearts. When I asked Joab what this meant, he told me these conversations were known as lies. They did not echo in the soul because they were false. To my astonishment, he continued that lies on Terra were common because humans did not trust one another. "Why?" I wanted to know. "Because they think only of themselves," he answered, "and their sole motivation is to satisfy their basic instincts and desires. This is the terrible tragedy of this race. It is called egotism. You must try to avoid its influence because it destroys everything it touches."

As predicted by Joab and Jeremiah, as soon as I started to speak the language of Terra and to participate more actively in my surroundings, a part of my consciousness began to fade. The world of illumination my guides inhabited grew opaque, and their voices became inaudible. One morning I awoke with no other memory than that of a child of Terra, one and a half years old. After this my life became more complicated. I had no one to explain the strange things I saw and heard on a daily basis. The women who took care of me did nothing but see to my meals and surround me with things I might find of interest. I was bored all the time. My only moments of happiness were spent with my father, who returned to my side as soon as my mother lost interest in me.

Sometimes my father would be absent for prolonged periods in order to do battle with our enemies, or so he told me. When he returned, he would always bring me wonderful and rare objects from his campaigns and would spend much of his time at my side to compensate for the time he was away. My mother and father avoided each other as much as possible, but when they came face to face, their arguments and mutual recriminations would terrify me. My screams would always silence them, but it was always my father who left the room.

My infancy passed quickly, and when I was just five years old, my father taught me how to use the lance and the short sword. One of his favorite distractions was to have me square off with a slave much older than I, instructing him to attack me as if I were an adult. This slave had been well trained in the martial arts and was highly valued by my father. I faced him without fear, my small feet firmly planted on either side of my naked body, my torso covered in scaled-down gold armor and a helmet of colored plumes on my tousled head. In my left arm, I held a gold shield, engraved with the rays of the sun. In my right arm, I held the short sword, ready to do battle.

Again and again the slave and I would clash in this uneven struggle. In the beginning, he would always win, oftentimes knocking the sword out of my hands with one swift move. Each time this happened, my father would punish me with his silence and an absence of several days. To me this was worse than a whipping by the slaves. I loved my mother, but there were no great ties of affection between us. My father, however, I adored with a bitter passion that made it hard for me to live when I could not see him.

After a few months of constant practice, the slave could no longer disarm me. By the age of seven, I could disarm him in seconds. I know my father was proud of my achievement, but he never let me see it. I only knew it because he visited me daily when he was not away and constantly brought beautiful gifts. He watched my diet carefully and made sure that I was never given any sweets. The only sweets I was allowed were fruits and their nectars. My mother brought me confections of honey and nuts, but when my father discovered this, his wrath was so great I thought he would strike her. I never saw my father so enraged. He screamed at her that she was trying to destroy all the work he had done, that she was weakening me and treating me like a girl. Warriors did not eat honey cakes, he bellowed. Sometimes they spent days or weeks with nothing at all to eat. My mother screamed back that I was not a warrior yet, but merely a child not quite eight. My father smashed his helmet against the floor in disgust and stormed out of the room with his soldiers. From that moment on, I refused to eat the sweets my mother brought me, and after a time she stopped bringing them altogether.

Perhaps to nullify the influence of my mother, my father hired a tutor for me, a skeletal and hateful creature named Leonidas. His job was to tutor me in the art and strategy of war. He was severe and crude and chastised me without mercy. He would force me to rise before dawn and order me to march around the grounds for hours before allowing me a breakfast so meager that even a Spartan would have complained. The afternoon was spent doing military exercises. This was followed by a small lunch and another exhausting march that culminated in dinner, an equally austere affair. Day after day I endured this boring and arduous routine without the enjoyment of playthings or distractions of any kind. My father visited me every day, obviously pleased with my progress, and I never complained, fearing to disappoint him. My mother, always ill-received by Leonidas and despised by my father, visited me only on rare occasions. Tightly enveloped in this cold and emotionally deprived atmosphere, I passed my childhood with nary a caress nor a moment of joy.

As the years passed, my father—who was a keen observer despite his increasing absences and growing fondness for wine and women—realized that by putting me under the sole tutelage of Leonidas, he had neglected my intellectual development in favor of the martial spirit. Therefore he dismissed Leonidas and hired a different tutor in order to remedy the situation. But before he did this, he decided to ensure that I would never forget that, above all else, I was to be a warrior. To this purpose, he presented me with the most magnificent of gifts, a great white horse so beautiful and spirited as to be a marvel to all who beheld him. I immediately named him Bucephalus, a word that meant "head of a bull," and indeed his head was enormous, as befitted his great intelligence.

When my father's slaves brought the horse to me, kicking and snorting, visible clouds of vapor issuing from his great nostrils, my heart filled with joy. I waited a few moments for them to bring him closer so that I could mount him, but he was not about to allow himself to be mounted or dominated by anybody. Observing that this magnificent beast seemed to fear the shadows created by his own movements, I grabbed his halter fearlessly and turned him away from the sun, speaking softly to him all the while. When he calmed down, I jumped on his back, and he did not throw me. In a short while, I was riding back and forth along the terrace of the palace atop Bucephalus as if we had been fused with each other. I had just turned thirteen. During the next seventeen years, Bucephalus would be my companion in all the great struggles of my life. When he finally died, ancient and covered with glory, I built a great city over his tomb and named it Bucephala.

Delighted with my equestrian prowess, my father took me the next day to meet my new tutor. This teacher was young, with a noble face and eyes full of serenity. He had been the disciple of one of the most admired men in Greece, and although he was as yet not well known, his reputation was growing because of his keen intelligence and his great understanding of science, art, and philosophy. His name was Aristotle.

My first impression of Aristotle was favorable, and despite the fact that anyone would have been preferable to the hateful Leonidas, my new teacher soon proved to be gentle and understanding without sacrificing firmness. My life changed completely from that time on. Something in Aristotle's clear gaze stirred in my soul deeply submerged memories of luminous faces and voices in the wind. But these dim memories of Joab and Jeremiah were buried too deeply within my being, and all the wisdom of Aristotle could not bring them back to life.

Aristotle taught me to love science and nature and to use logic in my reasoning. It was he who taught me that it was more important for a king to dominate his emotions than his enemies. Such was the interest that he instilled in me for science that for many years afterward, I would still send him rare specimens of plant and animal life from my various campaigns.

One of the first things Aristotle realized when he first met me was that I needed the companionship of boys of my own age. Following his suggestion, my father chose three companions among the sons of his nobles who were close to my own age, and for the first time in my life, I had friends. Hefastion, one of these young boys, soon became more like a brother than a friend. In time he came to be almost like my own true self. I would not have been able to survive without him. It was the first time that I knew true friendship and sincere affection. In my terrible and solitary life, this friendship was to bring me much comfort and solace.

Aristotle also instilled in me a great love for literature. My favorite writer was Pindar, who still lived in Thebes, but I also loved the great epic by Homer called the *Iliad*, which described the war between Troy and the Grecian states. This last work greatly influenced my developing intellect, and through it I absorbed a great deal of the old Greek values and ideas. All through my life, I slept with a copy of this book under my pillow, alongside a small dagger.

My education under Aristotle ended abruptly at the age of sixteen, when I was forced to sit on my father's throne while he fought a long and arduous campaign in Byzantium, just south of Thrace. Many of the court nobles thought ruling the empire was too difficult a task for an adolescent who was still studying his grammar and arithmetic, but my mind and spirit had been conditioned by my father to assume the reins of power since early childhood, and I dispatched my office with great efficiency. Before the year was out, I had the opportunity to try out not only my father's royal crown but also his war helmet. The Maedi, a Thracian tribe that had long been subjugated to Macedonia, took advantage of my father's absence and rebelled against us. It was my first chance to assume a military command. My father's soldiers accepted my leadership without squabble, and I led them to the low hills where the rebels hid. We dispatched them swiftly. Following the example of my father, I settled there a city that I called Alexandropolis, the city of Alexander, one of the many that were to bear my name.

My father was so proud of my triumph over the Maedi that he immediately made me a general in his army. I was barely eighteen years old.

The relationship between my mother and my father continued to deteriorate. Eventually he became so infatuated with one of his noble's nieces that he divorced my mother to marry her. This was unnecessary because our laws allowed men to have as many wives as they wished, therefore the action was viewed by my mother and her family as a deliberate affront. For the first time in my life, I allied myself with my mother against my father. I felt that his divorce and marriage to another woman was not only an insult to our family but also a threat to my hopes of ascending the throne. I had already tasted the sweetness of glory and was anxious to exercise the reins of power once again. In barely eighteen years, I had forgotten all of Joab and Jeremiah's warnings against the destruction that power brings.

As soon as my father remarried, my mother left the palace, and I left with her. My father did not try to detain me, but his generals were quick to remind him that it was absurd to speak of a unified Greece when he was unable to unify his own family. With little enthusiasm, my father sent for me. I returned with equal reluctance. My childish adoration for him had long been replaced with resentment and disdain. I always despised men who were dominated by women, a pretentious affectation that was largely influenced by my Aristotelian training. To make matters worse, my father's new wife gave birth to a boy, who became at once another pretender to the throne. When my father was finally assassinated by one of his bodyguards, the only feeling I experienced was relief.

As soon as my father was dead, I declared myself the King of Macedonia. The army, with whom I was very popular, accepted me immediately and with great fanfare. The rest of my father's court, however, did not share their enthusiasm. Atalus, the uncle of my father's second wife, quickly claimed the throne for her infant son. I reacted swiftly by sending one of my personal guards to visit Atalus. The uncle was never seen again.

My mother, more ferocious and far less subtle than I, silenced the aspirations of my younger brother and his mother in a particularly grisly manner. Although I did not personally witness this, I was told by one of my slaves that my mother forced her rival to witness the brutal assassination of her child, then forced her to hang herself. Another slave told me that both mother and child had been boiled alive. I never knew the true version of the story, as I thought it indiscreet to broach the subject with my mother.

My young brother was not the only pretender to the throne. Several others tried to usurp the crown that was rightfully mine. Their aspirations were short-lived, and I was eventually recognized as the heir to the throne of Macedonia. It did not matter to me that I was able to achieve this victory only by spilling the blood of all my rivals. The desire for power had invaded my soul like a malignant growth, and it would remain with me for the rest of my life. I was twenty years old.

After my ascension to Philip's throne, I dedicated my full time to the unification of Greece. To achieve this it was necessary to annex the great city-states of Athens, Thebes, and Corinth, cities that had always rebelled and resisted my father. To accomplish this, I relied not only on brute force but also on the military tactics and strategies I had learned from my father, and the tools of logic and reason I had acquired from Aristotle. Athens and Corinth fell easily. Thebes, aflame with the oratory of Demosthenes, who hated Macedonia, refused to submit. History later condemned my actions against Thebes as the result of my rage at their resistance, but this is not true. Every military decision I ever made was based on logic and cold reasoning. I decided to destroy Thebes and make it an example to the rest of Greece because I wanted them to know that my goal was not merely one of conquest but one of unification, and that all who opposed me would perish. I therefore razed and burned the city to the ground and left nothing standing except the house of Pindar, whose poetry I so admired. Six thousand Thebans were executed, among them women and children, priests and invalids. The rest were sold off as slaves. In the end, not even the ashes remained. Thebes as a Greek city had ceased to exist.

Having achieved my goal to unify Greece, I turned my attention to Persia. Centuries before, Persian invaders led by Xerxes had invaded Greece and stolen countless of our treasures, annexing many cities in the process. During his reign, Philip II, my father, had always dreamed of invading Persia, now ruled by Darius III. He had wanted to regain our lost treasures and lands and avenge the Persian insolence. His early demise ended his dream. It was now my turn to take up this dream and cover myself with glory.

The army that accompanied me on this ambitious quest was composed of 30,000 foot soldiers and 5,000 cavalry. It was a minuscule force with which to attempt the conquest of the Persian empire, but I knew that many of the annexed Greek cities would recognize me as their deliverer and join me, increasing my host. I also knew that the Macedonian phalanx was the most powerful military machine the world had ever seen. Disciplined, dedicated, and courageous, my army had never lost a battle. The phalanx, conceived by my father's military genius, was made of rank after rank of soldiers marching shoulder to shoulder, using their united shields to protect the front, the sides, and the heads of the soldiers inside the moving structure. Together they formed a solid wall of shields and swords and huge Macedonian lances, all moving and thinking as one man. As they marched forward, any arrow, lance, or projectile directed at them would rebound off the joined shields. It was practically invincible. Despite this, I knew that victory would not be easy. But I was determined to achieve it.

Before leaving Greece, I visited the oracle at Delphi to ask the priestess of Apollo if my campaign against the Persians would be victorious. The pythoness, alleging that the day was not propitious, refused to consult the oracle. I quickly grabbed her by the hair and put my dagger to her throat, repeating my request. Trembling, she answered, "My son, do you need ask? You know that you are invincible."

The words of the pythoness stayed with me throughout my long campaign against Persia and my struggle against Darius. In reality, she was right, for I never doubted my eventual triumph. It was as if I were obsessed with victory and carried within me a devouring fire that drove me to conquer.

To reach Persia I had to cross the Hellespont, which connected East and West. My small fleet caused much amusement and derision among the great Phoenician navy, who saw us cross the water from afar. So insignificant we must have seemed that they did not deign to pursue us, probably conjecturing that Darius's great army of over one million would quickly annihilate us. They could have never imagined that not only the Persians but they themselves would soon lie under my sandal.

The first thing I did upon reaching land was to visit Ilium, the ancient city of Troy, where the great ten-year Trojan War had taken place. I still carried with me Homer's poem relating the great deeds of Achilles, from whom I traced my lineage. A visit to this sacred site was for me the equivalent of a religious pilgrimage.

Together with my inseparable friend, Hefastion, I stood before the tombs of Achilles and his friend Patroclus and rendered homage to their memory. I then deposited my golden shield at the feet of Athena, substituting it for one that had been worn in that legendary war.

My first encounter with the Persians took place by the shores of the river Granicus. Darius, disdaining battle, sent one of his generals, Memnon, to face me. Memnon, a Greek, knew full well what he was up against and beseeched Darius to raze the towns and crops that surrounded my army so that we would starve to death, but Darius refused. That was the first of his many mistakes.

As soon as I arrived at the edge of the river, I entered the waters. Leading my cavalry, with my brilliant armor and the white plumes of my helmet visible for a mile, I directed the attack. Behind me, the infantry, led by my general Parmenio, moved forward with slow but fierce determination through the turbulent current of the river.

As soon as we reached the other side, the battle began in earnest. My initial blow with my lance was so strong that it broke in half. I quickly grabbed another and threw myself against the Persian commander, Mithridates, son-in-law to Darius. Taking advantage of my broken lance, he flung his javelin at me, which pierced not only my shield but also my armor. I escaped injury only because the javelin was light.

Furious at the destruction of my Trojan shield, I fell upon Mithridates, making Bucephalus leap over the bodies of the fallen. My first blow unseated him, and with my second, I drove my sword into his heart.

One of the Persian generals, seeing Mithridates fall, struck me a blow with his sword that split my helmet in half and opened my head to the bone in the process. Bathed in my own blood, I spun around and killed him instantly. Seeing me stagger, Mithridates's brother galloped toward me, sword raised, ready to finish me off. But my childhood friend, Cleitus, as much a brother to me as Hefastion, was nearby. He quickly swung his sword and cut off my attacker's arm in one motion. One moment later I fell unconscious to the ground.

The battle continued around me as I lay on the blood-soaked earth in a dead faint. Cleitus and Hefastion protected my body while my physician tried to stop the blood that flowed from my head like a fountain. As soon as he had bandaged my head and I had regained consciousness and was able to stand, I jumped back on Bucephalus and rejoined the battle with renewed furor.

When Memnon saw that his cause was lost, he withdrew his troops and sent me an emissary of peace. But I was filled with blood lust and the desire for victory and was in no mood to give quarter. In a few short hours, we tore the enemy to pieces. My principal anger was directed at the

Greek mercenaries who had joined Darius's army and betrayed our cause. Thousands of them perished, and the two thousand or so that survived were sent back as slaves to the mines of Macedonia. My losses were less than one hundred and fifty men. I always took care of my men, but remembering some long-forsaken lessons, I had the fallen Persians buried with full military honors. According to ancient legends, in this way I ensured a peaceful entry for them into the next world. My actions were deemed extraordinarily generous by both my men and the Persians.

The news of this first victory spread like wildfire among the annexed Greek cities along the coast of Asia Minor. One by one, they welcomed me as their deliverer.

In the spring of the following year, I reached Gordium, where my soldiers were able to rest and I consolidated my new armies. One of the famous legends of this region was that of the Gordian knot that was tied to the yoke of an old wagon by King Gordius of Phrygia. It was so huge and intricate that no one had ever been able to undo it. Legend said that he who was able to untie the Gordian knot would one day become the emperor of all Asia. Hundreds of men had tried to accomplish the feat without success.

Naturally, as soon as I heard this legend, I determined to untie the knot. It was precisely this kind of legend that served to inflame the imagination of the populace and make their conquest that much easier.

When I came face to face with the knot, I realized the enormity of the task before me. The knot was made up of hundreds of loops, each of which doubled around its circumference, which was as thick as Bucephalus's torso. The rope from which it was made was as thick as my ankle. I contemplated the phenomenon for a few minutes in silence. I knew it was impossible to undo it with my hands because along with its thickness, the years had hardened the rope, making it stiff and unyielding.

When the news spread that I was to try the knot, both my soldiers and the people of Gordium quickly gathered at the site to witness the spectacle. I could hear an occasional snicker among the crowd. They had all come to see the great Alexander, conqueror of so many armies, be defeated by a simple knot. Finally, tired of searching for the beginning of the knot, I shouted, "Who cares how it comes undone?" And with that, I drew out my sword and split the knot in half with one blow. At that instant, the sky roared with thunder and lightning, and a great cry of victory rose from the throats of my soldiers. From that moment on, everyone was convinced that I was a divine messenger.

But the adoration of my soldiers and the breaking of the Gordian knot was not the kind of glory that I had come to find in Persia. I was there to ascend the Persian throne, and to accomplish that, I had to face Darius.

Our first confrontation took place in the autumn of that same year, at the battle of Issus. When it began, our forces were equally matched, but the ferocity of our attack and our determination to triumph routed the Persian king and his generals. It was not long before his ranks were broken, his cavalry demolished, and the majority of his troops killed or taken prisoner. Once again, I urged Bucephalus to jump over the corpses of the enemy and sped across the battlefield toward the carriage that I knew to be Darius's. But the Persian king saw me approaching, and he must have seen death in my eyes because he leapt out of his carriage and into a smaller conveyance, which took off immediately. I gave chase for several miles, but he disappeared into the night.

Darius's flight signaled the complete demoralization of his remaining troops, who surrendered to me immediately. Accompanied by Cleitus and Hefastion, I picked up the mantle and shield Darius had abandoned and strode over to the royal tents where I knew his family waited.

When they saw me enter with Darius's mantle and shield, both his mother and his wife thought he was dead. With cries of terror, they threw themselves at my feet and asked for mercy for themselves and Darius's daughters. I was always gallant with women and strictly forbade my soldiers to rape or abuse the women of conquered cities. With great gentleness, I lifted the two women to their feet and assured them they had nothing to fear at my hands, and that I would always treat them as the royal Persian family. And even though it was my right as conqueror to take Darius's wife for my own, I never laid a hand on her. His mother, Sisygambis, grew to be one of my most loyal friends. Jeremiah later told me that upon my death, she turned her face to the wall, refusing to speak or eat until she died.

But Darius was still free, and while he was at large, I could claim neither his throne nor his crown. Aware of the vastness of the empire he controlled and the great wealth it encompassed, I decided to continue my pursuit. Before this, however, I had to ensure that my own throne was safe back in Macedonia. In order to achieve this, I launched an attack on Tyre, the great fortified city of the Phoenecians that was the principal center of commerce on the Mediterranean. Once I had Tyre in my grasp, I knew that I could control the entire Mediterranean coast and thus be able to repel any attacks on Greece.

I began my first assault on Tyre with diplomacy. I sent various emissaries of peace to the commander of their garrison, asking that they join with me and avoid the shedding of blood. But the leaders of Tyre were sure that the walls of their city were impregnable. Their answer to me was the assassination of my emissaries, whose bodies were thrown over the city ramparts.

I understood the message and prepared for battle. In order to breach their walls, I needed to use catapults along with battering rams, but their walls had their foundation deep in the water, and the use of catapults required firm ground.

This apparent obstacle did not deter me in my determination to conquer Tyre. If firm ground was required to use the catapults, I would create firm ground. With nary a second thought, I called together my generals and informed them of my plan: We were to build a road across the waters from which we would attack Tyre. This ambitious and difficult plan was put into effect immediately. The construction of the road took six months, during which my troops endured with impassive fortitude a constant barrage of rocks and other projectiles thrown down at us by the Phoenicians, who knew exactly what that road meant.

On the very day the road was finished, we raised our catapults and, with the help of the battering rams, made short work of the proud Queen of the Mediterranean. What Nebuchadnezzar, the great King of Babylonia, had been unable to accomplish, I achieved with my tenacity and intelligence. The coast of the Mediterranean was mine. I had fulfilled my father's dream.

When Darius, still in hiding, heard of this new triumph, he wrote to me immediately, offering me the western half of his empire, ten thousand talents, and the hand of one of his daughters in marriage. Jeremiah later told me that had I accepted this offer, Hellenic culture would have stagnated in Persia. As it was, Darius's missive only made me laugh and I rejected it contemptuously.

In the meantime, I continued my quest to bring the art, philosophy, and great culture of my homeland to the rest of the ancient world, from where it would pass on to Rome and the rest of the world.

From Tyre, I went on to Egypt, which I conquered with no great effort. The Egyptians accepted me with open arms and not only made me Pharaoh but declared me a living god. This did not surprise me in the least. My mother had always told me that it had been one of the Olympian gods that had engendered me, not Philip of Macedonia. I behaved with great largesse toward the Egyptians, fortifying their cities, solving their flood and irrigation problems, and allowing them to continue to worship their ancient gods. Furthermore, I declared that their god Ammon was the same as the god Zeus, the supreme god of the Greeks. If a Creator exists, I told them—and of that there is no doubt, He must have created Himself—there can be only one god, but He has many names. This statement earned for me the eternal love and veneration of the Egyptians.

But the most important thing by far that I did in Egypt was to found the city of Alexandria. Because it bore my name, I had to make it the most beautiful and rich city in the world. Alexandria was only one of seventy cities that bore my name, but it is the only one that still exists on Terra. It was the first completely modern city, constructed on a pattern of wide avenues crossed by narrower streets. Alexandria soon replaced Tyre as the main commercial center of the region and quickly became the foremost international city of its time. Greeks, Persians, Indians, Jews, and all nations came to call at its ports.

Darius wrote to me again, this time raising his offer to twenty thousand gold talents. Again I rejected the offer and instead engaged him in battle once more. This time we faced each other in Gaugamela, where I once again defeated Darius, who managed to escape a second time.

My next campaign was against Babylonia. It ended quickly and victoriously. I spent the next month relaxing by the Hanging Gardens of Nebuchadnezzar with my friends, Cleitus and Hefastion, and the rest of my troops. After Babylon, I conquered Susa and Persepolis, the capital of the Persian Empire. These conquests netted me a fortune of nearly two hundred thousand gold talents.

Persepolis was to the Persians what Jerusalem was to the Jews and Mecca was to the Muslims. It was the sacred city of Darius's empire. To make sure that the Persians and their fugitive king understood that their empire no longer existed, I ordered my men to sack and raze the city. I then burned the royal palace and ordered a palace of my own to be erected. Never would I sleep under my enemy's roof.

Darius continued to elude me, and I determined at last to find him or perish trying. I finally cornered him in the small city of Ecbatana in the Kurdish mountains. But Darius evaded me till the end. Before I could get to him, Bessus, one his generals, assassinated him. When I finally stood before Darius's body, I covered it with my mantle and sent it to his mother for burial.

Bessus then had the great audacity to crown himself Artaxerxes IV, king of Persia, something that I would have found amusing had I not been in such a hurry. I postponed my next campaign and hunted him down. When I found him, I had his nose and his ears cut off in the Persian manner and then sent him to Ecbatana to stand trial for treason. The Persians and the Medes found him guilty and sentenced him to be quartered alive.

After the death of Darius, I decided to invade Iran, which I also accomplished easily. Shortly after this I wed a young

Bactrian princess named Roxana. I did not love her; our marriage was a political maneuver intended as a conciliatory gesture toward her father and her people. I also needed an heir to my throne, and I knew that marriage to a Persian woman would consolidate my support with the Persians.

My marriage to Roxana was ill received by both my troops and my friends. They thought I was becoming too influenced by oriental culture and was forgetting my Greek roots. Little by little, I isolated myself from my friends and my men. I started to doubt and suspect everyone around me. I was sure that someone was trying to murder me.

My suspicions and fears grew daily, centering finally on the son of my oldest and most trusted general, Parmenio. In order to stop this imagined conspiracy, I ordered the assassination of the youth. Not content with this murder, I also ordered the assassination of his father, fearing his reprisals. Parmenio was over seventy years old and the most popular of my generals. My men never forgave me for his death.

Following this unpardonable crime, my mind continued its precipitous descent. I had always been abstemious before, but now I began to drink nightly, so heavily that I often passed out on the floor. I felt alone and lost. During a celebration with the few friends I had left, Cleitus, my old childhood friend, who had saved my life at the battle of Granicus, dared criticize me. Blinded by wine and rage, I took out my sword and ran him through. Cleitus fell to the ground without a word, dying instantly.

The murder of this faithful friend filled me with such remorse that I took to my bed for three days and refused to eat. In the end my doctors convinced me that this terrible action had not been my fault because it had been the result of a divine madness. This helped ease my conscience and alleviate my sorrow, but it did not deter my downfall. I became a despot and a tyrant. Even my old teacher, Aristotle, spoke ill of me.

My next and final campaign led me to India, where I met the holy men known as gurus, one of whom accompanied me throughout what was left of my life. In India my troops finally rebelled, refusing to accompany me any further in the tropical rains. They knew I had no intention of returning to Greece until I had conquered the entire world. They were weary and battle scarred, and all they wanted to do was return to Greece and hang up their swords. For two days I sequestered myself in my tent, angry and embittered that my dreams of conquest had come to an end. I knew my men deserved this long-awaited rest, but I was by no means ready to end my dreams of glory. I was still determined not to stop my campaigns until the entire known world was under my rule. But I knew this dream could not be fulfilled without the willing support of my troops. Therefore I decided to relent and agree to their demands. I knew how to wait. After a suitable rest, I would again embark in the last and most glorious of my campaigns. Sooner or later the whole world would be at my feet. Having arrived at this decision, I emerged from my tent with a broad smile on my face and told my chief marshall Coenus, who spoke on the troops' behalf, that I agreed to their petition. The troops applauded the decision, and the next day we started on our way back to Persia.

This return was by no means easy, being fraught with rebellions within my ranks, disease, and the death of many of my men, some of it caused by the destructive power of the Indian monsoon. Once again in the city of Susa, the administrative center of the Persian Empire, I determined to fuse

Macedonians and Persians into a master race. To carry this policy further, I married one of Darius's daughters, Barsine, while my friend Hefastion married the other, Drypetis. Ten thousand of my men and eighty of my officers followed my example and married Persian women.

This decision was met with open antagonism by the Macedonians in my army, who openly threatened mutiny. Tired and disgusted with the whole lot of them, I dismantled the entire army and sent them packing back to Greece. But I was careful to present them with much gold and costly gifts in order to silence them forever. The ruse worked, and the crisis was surmounted. Once I was rid of them, I proceeded to rebuild my army, this time composed entirely of Persians, whom I found much easier to manipulate. But I was already weak and exhausted, my body wracked by the pain of ancient wounds.

It was during this time that destiny dealt me the greatest pain of my life. My beloved friend Hefastion died of a sudden fever. His death destroyed what was left of my health. For three days I locked myself with the body, refusing to abandon him. When I finally came out of the funeral chamber, I ordered the execution of his physician, accusing him of incompetence. Hefastion's funeral was the grandest in the history of our times, but I never recovered from his loss.

Several months after his death, I fell ill after a prolonged drinking spree. My doctors did not know what to make of my illness, although some suspected malaria. Rumors also spread that I had been poisoned, but it was not so. What killed me was grief over the death of Hefastion and remorse for the murders of Cleitus and Parmenio. They were the only friends I had known in my whole life; theirs was the only affection that had illuminated my spirit. Neither my mother nor my father nor any of my wives had been able to touch my soul or enter my heart. My only child was yet unborn and thus unable to show me love.

On the thirteenth day of June of the year 323 B.C., at exactly six in the evening, my troubled soul was finally freed of matter and returned to its spiritual state. Legend later said that a great lightning bolt had risen from the sea and stretched out toward heaven, carrying in its center an eagle and a star. When the star disappeared from view, I closed my eyes forever. I lived only thirty-three years on Terra. During my lifetime I was emperor and master of the entire world, even a god to some, yet I never knew happiness, and no one cried at my death.

My empire was divided among my generals. My first wife, Roxana, assassinated my second wife, Barsine, the daughter of Darius. Later on, one of her enemies assassinated her, my young son, and my mother Olympias. There was no one left of my lineage or my bloodline on the planet. It was as if the Creator had decided that my seed should be extinguished with my death.

How right Jeremiah and Joab had been when they foretold a life filled with suffering and destruction on Terra! And yet I did not regret the experience. I committed many errors and innumerable crimes; I was cruel, despotic, and ruthless; and I abused my power often and without pity. I had no excuse for these crimes except the weakness of my flesh. Yet my intentions had been noble, and despite my many failures, my mission had not been a total loss. I gave Terra the concept of unification, a revolutionary idea at the time, and I extended the frontiers of civilization from Greece to India. I illuminated the world with Aristotelian logic, and I enriched it with literature, art, and the Hellenic sciences. For these accomplishments, human history named me Alexander the Great, but this did not end my pilgrimage. Many centuries had yet to pass before I could again meet with Verdigris.

§

after death

what happens

purification

what happens

after death

6 THE EXPERIENCE OF DEATH AS

a human being was completely different from what I had felt till then. The personality of Alexander, so strong and indomitable, had clung to life like a tiger to its prey. At the moment of death, delirious as I was with fever, I was completely unaware of what was happening around me. All I knew was that life, as sweet as it was bitter, was escaping me as slowly as water evaporating under the rays of the sun. I tried to hold on to it desperately. Despite all I had suffered, I wanted to live. There were still worlds to conquer, battles to win. But my breath was failing me, and my heart fluttered like the wings of a sparrow, weak and tired of beating.

I felt a slight pull, and suddenly I was outside of my body, almost as if I had become disconnected from it. I was not breathing, yet I did not seem to need to. My body felt light and comfortable, and a delicious languor invaded my senses. My fever had disappeared along with all the pain my body had endured for such a long time. At that moment, it did not matter who I was or what was going to happen. I was completely happy and satisfied.

Slowly, without any conscious effort, I started to float toward the ceiling. Below me, I could see my physicians and several of my officers looking at my inert body. I could hear them talking among themselves, but their conversation did not interest me. Neither did I find it strange that I could see my body down on the bed while I was floating up near the ceiling. It was as if I were watching a scene in a play that had nothing to do with me.

Suddenly I felt a stronger pull toward one of the corners of the ceiling, and the sound of many crystal bells rang deeply within me. I was enveloped in a blanket of soothing darkness as I rushed outwardly toward the cosmos and lost total awareness of myself.

When I regained consciousness, I was once again in the vestibule of souls with Joab and Jeremiah. All my previous existences passed rapidly before my eyes as if I were living them over again. I understood at that moment that I was not Alexander, but a free spirit with no material ties. The memory of Verdigris returned to me with overwhelming yearning.

"Not yet." The guides' answer came to me subtly and simultaneously.

"When?" I asked bitterly. "How much longer must I wait?"

"It depends on you," they answered. "You have wasted a long time because you keep ignoring the instructions you receive before each existence."

"But I don't ignore them!" I protested.

"Why then did you allow yourself to be influenced so profoundly by vanity and selfishness during your existence as Alexander? We warned you not to allow yourself to fall into their clutches," admonished Jeremiah.

"But you said that as I became involved with the influences of Terra, the memory of your teachings would fade."

"That is not what we told you," corrected Joab. "What we said was that you would lose contact with us and would be unable to perceive us because of the terrestrial influence, but we also told you that while the body may forget the lessons, the soul never does. All you had to do was think carefully before acting, and the submerged teachings would have resurfaced to illuminate your decisions. But you acted rashly all your life, seldom weighing the consequences of your destructive and cruel actions. You did not forget your lessons, you simply ignored them because power and glory obscured your reason. It was easier to indulge your vanity and selfishness than to put your pride in check and control your physical instincts."

The memory of my life as Alexander returned to me at that instant along with deep remorse for all my brutal actions. I recalled with horror my persecution of Darius, my rejection of his desire for peace, and his humiliating death at the hands of a traitor. My bloody memories continued to fall like a molten waterfall on my terrified soul, choking me in their pestilent miasma. I remembered my arrogant decision to destroy the Macedonian mercenaries who had joined the Persian army because I judged them traitors to the Greek cause, while years later I would disband my entire Greek army and embrace the Persian lifestyle, abandoning my culture and my roots. What hypocrisy and selfish disregard for my own people! But of all these bitter memories, the deaths of Cleitus and Parmenio were the hardest to accept. I understood then that Joab and Jeremiah were correct in their judgment. Throughout my entire life as Alexander, I always knew when my actions had been dictated by necessity and when they were motivated by selfishness. The lessons my guides had taught me had not been forgotten; they had been assimilated by my spirit, and I knew right from wrong. It was pride and arrogance, not ignorance of the Law, that had guided my actions as Alexander.

"Forgive me!" I cried in anguish. "I now realize my terrible guilt. I deserve the worst of punishments for my crimes!"

"Why do you continue to think about punishment?" asked Jeremiah sadly. "There is no punishment. Each soul passes through several lives in order to experience matter, to learn new lessons; but because matter is dense and corruptive, purification is necessary in the measure in which the soul corrupts itself. Souls interact and often act as each other's athanors to effect purification. Some spirits advance more rapidly than others in their path of experiential search, but eventually they all return to the Light whence they originated. When a soul falls into the trap of identifying with the material world completely, breaking one or more of the Cosmic Laws in the process, it must be purified through sorrow and self-sacrifice in the course of many existences. That is why sorrow and self-sacrifice are such important lessons. As long as you reject them, you reject purification."

"How many more lives must I experience before I can be purified from my existence as Alexander?"

The light from my two guides flickered slightly, then the answer arrived from both of them simultaneously.

"It is true that as Alexander you committed many crimes, but you also did much that was good. Your vision and generosity made possible the exchange of ideas between different cultures, and your contributions to the evolution of future generations was immense. These things must also be taken into consideration."

"But surely I must pay for all the lives I destroyed—Darius, Cleitus, Parmenio."

"The lives you destroyed in battle were the result of a struggle between antagonists bent on mutual destruction. It is the way in which inferior species cancel each other out, by allowing only the strongest to survive. If you had not destroyed your foes, they would have destroyed you. Both of you went into battle knowing this. Therefore you exonerated each other from the responsibility of your mutual deaths. Darius's death falls in that group. Cleitus and Parmenio were victims of your arrogance and egotism. Those deeds have to be atoned for and purified. All the destruction you left in your wake, your vanity and your pride, these also have to be eradicated so that your soul can advance on your evolutionary path. How long it will take depends entirely on you."

The words of my guides filled me with joy. In spite of my anguish, I saw hope for purification as the ultimate aim of my soul.

"I will attempt to complete this mission as swiftly as possible," I said humbly. "I will embrace sorrow and self-sacrifice as the most precious of friends. I have accepted the lesson, and I will never forget it."

"In this next lifetime, you will meet again with the spirits of Parmenio and Cleitus, whom you have to repay for the crimes you committed against them," said Joab. "They will be your athanors in this new existence, and through them you could be purified completely of material corruption. But it is your decision. Are you willing to undergo this experience? It will be the most painful of all your existences."

"I am willing," I answered at once, impatient to start my new adventure.

"So be it," said Jeremiah gravely. "Terra has been chosen as the place where you will experience matter during the rest of your spiritual evolution. It is a most difficult place for a soul to overcome the temptations of matter. That is why every existence on Terra is a great test of the spirit. If you can overcome the basic instincts of your terrestrial body, you can advance very quickly there and meet Verdigris that much sooner."

These words made my resolve stronger, but my spirit still had one persistent doubt.

"How can I ensure that the lessons I have learned will not be rejected by this new incarnation?"

"Function through your spirit and not the physical body," answered Joab. "The body is transient and impermanent. It is an illusion of the senses. Never allow it to dominate your spirit."

"And how can I accomplish this?"

"By sacrificing for others, and giving to others what you most want for yourself," interposed Jeremiah. "Only by giving of yourself will you be able to dominate matter. Rest now," he added tenderly. "When you awake, you will be back on Terra."

Suspended in the light that permeated the vestibule of souls like a radiant cloud, I sank slowly into the healing sleep in which the spirit regains its energies prior to entering a new life. All around me, the tenuous shapes of other souls floated on shimmering rows that extended into the infinite. They also were enjoying the ephemeral blessing of spiritual rest.

§

after death

what happens

sacrifice and forgiveness

what happens

after death

7 **DURING THE FIRST TWO YEARS**
of my second existence on Terra, Joab and Jeremiah were constantly with me. Even when I began to talk and walk, they remained beside me. But the day came when their beloved presence began to fade once more in the face of human dialogue, and then I perceived them no longer.

My suffering in this life started when I barely had use of reason. This time I was born into the beautiful city of Kalinga, situated in the Bay of Bengal in the magical and mysterious land known as India. At the time of my birth, the nation was still ruled by the caste system, and to expiate my pride during my previous existence, it was my sad fate to be born into the fifth and lowest caste, the despised Pariahs, or Untouchables. My name was Chandra.

My parents and I lived in a miserable shanty with two tiny rooms. The front room served as a kitchen, dining area, and living quarters, while the back room served as the bedroom. The floor was made of hard earth. My poor mother cooked the minuscule amounts of food my father obtained through whatever odd job he was able to get from a nearby farmer. This man belonged to the Sudra caste, which was only just one step above our own and almost as equally despised, yet he took joy in humiliating and degrading my father at every chance he had. He gave my father the basest jobs, such as cleaning the cesspools or the sewers. The pay my father received from this menial work was so small that we were barely able to eat.

Shortly after my first birthday, my sister Ayida was born; she was followed the next year by Narda, and two years later by Dakmar. If we were nearly starving when we were only three, the birth of my sisters considerably worsened the situation. When my brothers Parsis, Gupta, and Kanishka were born, it was necessary for me to go begging into the streets in order to help my family. I was barely nine years old when I started to beg, but given my state of malnutrition, I appeared much younger. My skin barely covered my bones, which in turn were barely covered by the rags that served as my only clothes. Once in a while, the matrons of the city would take pity on my age and feeble appearance and would throw me some coins or a bit of food from afar, but only as long as I did not go near them. Because of my Untouchable condition, the mere brush of my fingers would corrupt them, as was India's belief at the time.

The largesse of these ladies was infrequent, and what was most commonly thrown at me were stones, curses, and spittle. Nobody wanted Pariahs hanging about. I came home nearly every day covered by fresh bruises and saliva. My poor mother would cry her heart out seeing my condition, knowing that the next day I would have to go out again, in the hopes that amidst all the abuse, I would meet with some compassion.

Hunger and hard labor took the life of my consumptive father when I was barely twelve years old. My mother struggled tenaciously against the same terrible disease, terrified at the thought of what would happen to her small children if she also died. My youngest brother was not yet two years old.

Knowing that I was the sole support of my family sharpened my instincts and my natural intelligence, and I always found a way to bring something home. After a while, I learned a clever trick from one of the beggars of my own caste. We would go to one of the many market stalls in the city and touch the food and vegetables that were displayed on the streets. This immediately made the produce inedible, as it had been corrupted by Untouchables, and the shopkeepers would throw the food out into the street, where we would pick it up. It was a good system, but it soon became so popular that the shopkeepers began to set up guard by their wares or keep them inside their stores where they were out of our reach. I was left once more to my own devices in my search for food, and hunger returned to our family.

One day as I walked around the city I found myself straying farther away from the area where I normally begged and getting nearer the royal palace, which until now I had seen only from afar. Careful not to be seen by the guards who patrolled the grounds, I cautiously circled the magnificent sculpted wall that enclosed the splendid edifice. Entranced, I peered at the marvelous gardens that could be seen through the designs on the wall. Suddenly I noticed a narrow opening in the wall that was part of its design. Without thinking twice, I climbed through it and found myself within the gardens.

Hiding behind the fragrant jasmine bushes, I made my way around the garden, never straying too far from the wall in case I had to beat a hasty retreat. After a short while, I caught the delicious scent of food coming from one of the side buildings. Throwing caution to the wind, I let myself be guided by the smell until I reached the doors of the palace kitchen. Nearly fainting from hunger, I stretched out my hand to push open the door, and found myself face to face with a huge man of imposing stature and graying whiskers.

This frightening apparition left me paralyzed with terror, and there I would have stayed if a gigantic hand had not grabbed me by the neck and pulled me inside the building. When I recovered my wits, I realized that I was in a larder filled with more food than I ever knew existed. The man who dragged me inside the building introduced himself as Siddhartha, the royal cook. He told me that my audacity could have cost me my life if the palace guards had found me. When I asked him which caste he belonged to, considering he had now touched a Pariah, he said he belonged to the Vaisya, or third caste, but that the caste system meant nothing to him because he had abandoned the Hindu religion to practice Buddhism.

"The castes are only recognized by the Hindus," he said. "But I follow the teachings of Buddha, who founded this new religion."

"What kind of religion ignores the castes and makes equals of an Untouchable and a Vaisya?"

"The religion that states that all humans are equal and that none is more worthy than the other," he answered.

"Not even the Brahmans?" I asked in disbelief.

"Not even them," my new friend assured me with a smile.

In the ensuing course of our conversation, he explained that the Buddha, a name that means the "enlightened one," had originally been called Siddhartha like himself. But the Buddha had also been a prince, and his full name had been Siddhartha Gautama. This prince had abandoned his palace, his wife, and his child in pursuit of perfect truth, which he had found while sitting under a Bodhi tree. Through this enlightenment he had discovered that all the problems and suffering in this life are caused by avarice, jealousy, and egoism. From that moment on, he preached kindness, equality, and truth. According to Buddha, to be happy, a human being must forget himself or herself and live to serve others. Only in this way can a soul achieve the state of perfect peace and happiness known as Nirvana, if not in this lifetime, in the next, because Buddha also taught that all souls journey through a series of incarnations as they search for purification and the eventual bliss of Nirvana.

The teachings of Buddha that I heard for the first time from Siddhartha brought to my mind echoes of other teachings I had long forgotten. I knew that I had heard something similar as a child, but I could not remember where or from whom. The voices of Joab and Jeremiah had long ago disappeared from my consciousness.

My miserable condition as an Untouchable and the desperate circumstances of my family moved Siddhartha, who gave me a sack filled with exquisite delicacies and urged me to return the next day. Not to the kitchen, he warned, but to the other side of the bay, where he would be waiting for me with a new batch of provisions.

When I arrived at home, my arms filled with delicious foods, the likes of which we had never imagined, my family were beside themselves with excitement. It had been so long since they had eaten well that this banquet seemed like something out of a dream.

The next day, I arrived eagerly at the place Siddhartha had chosen. After I had waited for him a little while, he arrived with his arms full of packages and delicacies of every sort. After greeting me affectionately, we sat down by the water, and Siddhartha proceeded to continue the Buddhist instruction he had begun the day before.

These meetings continued daily for many months, and I always received nourishment not only for the body but also for the soul. Each day I grasped more fully the beautiful teachings of Buddha and grew to accept the unity of humanity and the need to sacrifice for others. My condition as an Untouchable no longer bothered me because I knew that it was only part of my karma, of a trial my spirit had to undergo, a lesson it had to learn. My present life would eventually pass, and there would be others during which I would be repaid for my suffering and good deeds.

Good nutrition and the medicines I was able to buy with the money Siddhartha occasionally gave me eased my mother's illness a great deal and brought back some color into my brothers' and sisters' cheeks. But nothing in life is permanent, and something in my heart told me that this ideal situation would come to an end sooner or later. I do not know how I knew this, but often I would awake in the middle of the night, drenched in icy sweat and my heart climbing out of my throat. I was so sure that something was about to happen that I began to hoard food like a squirrel. From the staples I received daily from Siddhartha, I would put away a good portion, hiding the food in an improvised pantry I set up in a corner of the room. My mother smiled gently at my concerned attitude and told me I was being overly cautious, but occasionally I noticed a look of anxiety flicker across her emaciated face.

The day I dreaded came finally, just as I knew it would. The fragile sense of security that had enveloped us with the help of my loyal friend was completely destroyed with one savage blow. Its cause was the invasion of Kalinga by the Mauryan emperor Asoka, who had dominated India for the last thirteen years.

The attack on Kalinga was so brutal that it left the city in ruins in a matter of hours. For many days, we huddled together in our hut while the screams of our less fortunate neighbors rang out all about us. For the first time in my life, I was glad to be an Untouchable, as the invaders belonging to the upper castes all but ignored the part of the city where my people lived.

My foresight in saving food in the expectation of a catastrophe was what saved our lives during those first terrible days. At the end of the first week, seeing that our supply was getting low, I decided to go out in search of more food. My hope was that the palace still stood and that Siddhartha was still the royal cook there. Following the suggestion of my mother, I brought along my brother Parsis, who, though being barely six years old, was very intelligent and had assimilated well the teachings of Buddha I had shared with him and my other siblings. Parsis did not know that castes existed in India because I had vowed to save him and my other brothers and sisters from the stigma of their heritage through the teachings of Buddha.

The desolation I found upon leaving our house was much worse than I had anticipated. Of the beautiful city of Kalinga, nothing remained except ashes and rubble. In our journey across the city, we found the destruction that was an integral part of all warfare: bodies charred by the heat of battle; children lost, crying for their mothers; mothers desperately seeking their children. Hunger, terror, pestilence, and death all joined together in an assault on the senses.

Horrified by the terrible spectacle, I decided to go straight to the palace in the hope of finding Siddhartha. As we walked along we saw no sign of the invaders, and I began to nurture the hope that they might have left the ruined city, but then I spotted the walls of the palace and a large retinue of armed men surrounding the structure. I knew at once they belonged to Asoka's army because their uniforms were different than those of the palace guards.

Little by little I drew closer to the soldiers, my brother Parsis holding on to my shirt. I was sure that our age would preclude any violence against us and hoped that our status as Untouchables might move someone to give us alms. When I had reached a certain distance from the palace, I noticed a tall man standing in front of the garden gate, wearing imposing robes of brocaded gold.

"That must be Asoka," I whispered to my brother. "I am sure he has decided to take possession of the royal palace. That is probably why he has not destroyed it."

"Do you think Siddhartha is still alive?" Parsis asked me.

"I do not know, but I doubt it," I answered sadly. "I do not think Asoka has allowed anyone from the palace to survive."

"He must be very powerful," said Parsis. "I have never seen clothes like that before. Chandra, do you think he will give us alms if we go up to him?"

I shook my head, knowing that an Untouchable could not go near a member of the elite caste of the Brahmans under penalty of death. But Parsis did not know anything about the caste system, much less that we were members of the most despised caste in India.

"I am going to ask him for alms," he said suddenly. "I am sure he will not refuse me."

And before I could stop him, he let go of my shirt and ran off to the group of soldiers surrounding Asoka.

"No, Parsis, wait!" I screamed in terror, knowing what awaited my little brother if he got too close to the Emperor. But Parsis ignored my call and continued to run toward

Asoka. Desperately I ran after him, but just as I reached his side, my worst fears were realized.

My brother, innocent of the destruction he was about to bring down upon himself, approached the great invader and, stretching out a small hand, picked up the hem of his garment and brought it to his lips. At that same instant, I arrived by his side. Everything that happened then transpired as if in a dream. The emperor turned to look at us. His face grew pale and then dark with rage. The soldiers who surrounded him had not been able to detain my brother, whose sudden action took them all by surprise. They now brought out their swords but did not use them. Horrified and revolted at the thought of an Untouchable kissing their emperor's robe, they drew back, stunned, and waited for Asoka's reaction.

Asoka's eyes burned with fury.

"Beast!" he bellowed, drawing a glimmering saber from the gold scabbard by his side. "How dare you place your impure hands on my person! Because of you, I am now as corrupt as you are, and must undergo purification before I can touch another of my caste. Prepare to die!"

Before the saber could fall on Parsis's head, I stepped forward in front of my brother.

"Mercy, your Majesty!" I cried desperately. "My brother is not to blame. It was I who touched your Majesty, not him!"

Asoka held his saber and glowered at me.

"So you admit what you have done," he roared. "Why did you dare do such a thing, knowing I am a Brahman?"

"Because I was hungry," I cried. "I was hoping for some alms. I forgot your caste."

"I will make sure you remember it in the future," Asoka rumbled. "Stretch out your hands!"

Trembling with fear, I extended my hands.

The saber fell like a silver half-moon over my arms, and a river of blood surged from where my hands had been a moment before. In a trance, I heard a scream escape my brother's throat.

"It was I, my Lord, it was I!" Parsis screamed, his body wracked with sobs. "It wasn't my brother, it was me. Cut off my hands too!" And he extended his small hands for the Emperor to sever.

Asoka stared at us for a moment, and his face drained of color.

"Is it true that it was not you who touched me?" he asked.

I had fallen on my knees by his feet, my arms numb from the elbows down. I felt no pain, but the loss of blood, along with my malnutrition, was clouding my eyes and my mind.

"No, Majesty, it was not me," I said, barely conscious. "But my brother is innocent. No one has ever taught him the difference between the castes. He only knows the teachings of Buddha that say we are all equal. That is why he dared touch you. To him we are all brothers, and compassion reigns in the human heart. Forgive him, Sire, have mercy."

Through a thickening fog, I heard the emperor call to his soldiers.

"Quickly, someone stop the flow of his blood. And bring my physician."

But no one moved to obey him. I continued to be an Untouchable, and no member of a higher caste was about to come near me, let alone save my life.

Asoka turned to my brother.

"You! Give me a hand!" With the aid of his saber, still stained with my blood, he cut pieces off his linen tunic and with Parsis's aid wrapped them tightly around the scarlet stumps at the end of my arms. Once he had finished bandaging my wounds, in front of the disbelieving eyes of his soldiers, he knelt by my fallen body and took my head in his hands.

"Forgive me," he said in trembling voice. "Forgive me. You are but a mere child, yet you have taught Buddha's lesson of selfless sacrifice."

"It is you who must forgive me," I answered. "In another life I did you a great injustice and took your life. Now that I am at the threshold of eternity, I remember it all. Do not be bitter about what has happened. It was karma we each had to fulfill. Only promise me that you will take care of my mother and my siblings."

"I promise," said Asoka. "Die in peace."

Those were the last words that I heard in my second existence on Terra.

§

after death

what happens

verdigris

what happens

after death

8 AS MY GUIDES HAD FORETOLD,

Chandra was the most painful and most illuminating of all my existences. For the first time in my evolutionary path, I had the spiritual clarity to remember other lives while still incarnated. Laying amongst the ruins of Kalinga with my head nestled in Asoka's arms, I felt my life seeping out of my body together with the blood that flowed like a river from my wounded arms. And at that moment, all my previous lives passed before my eyes, illuminating my consciousness with divine light. I remembered clearly my life as Alexander of Macedonia and the crimes that had condemned me to my terrible life as Chandra. In those agonizing moments, I perceived Asoka as he had been in that life: my general Parmenio, whose vile assassination I had ordered. My brother Parsis, for whom I had sacrificed my life, I recognized as my beloved friend Cleitus, whom I had killed in a moment of drunken rage.

Along with this awakening, I realized that for the first time in one of my incarnations, I had completely fulfilled the mission that had been assigned to me. A great sense of peace and joy descended upon me as I realized that I had greatly advanced in my long search for Verdigris.

In this spiritual exuberance, I surrendered my soul to the cosmos. I felt myself being lifted rapidly to places I had never known by a force of indescribable power. When I regained consciousness, I found myself suspended in a immense amphitheater formed by the brilliant light of a multicolored rainbow whose rays stretched into the infinite. Amidst that boundless radiance, I perceived two beings of light, Joab and Jeremiah. My spirit was suffused with transcendental joy upon perceiving my beloved guides, and their great love enveloped my soul in fragrant waves of peace.

"Rejoice!" they said in unison. "You have finally conquered matter!"

Trembling with emotion, I asked why I was not in the vestibule of souls. They answered that having accomplished my mission at last, there was no need to linger in my former place of rest, where souls only sojourned to replenish their energies and to await their next incarnation.

"What will happen now?" I asked.

"Now you will undergo your greatest test," answered Jeremiah. "You will return to Terra, where you will finally meet with Verdigris."

These long-awaited words overwhelmed my soul with an indescribable emotion, where rapture blended with bliss and terror; bliss at the thought of reuniting again with my beloved, and terror at the idea of a new catastrophe that would further delay that union.

"Verdigris! Am I really going to unite again with Verdigris?" I asked, my soul shivering with ecstasy.

Jeremiah's answer confirmed my fears.

"Union!" he said sternly. "I did not speak of union, only of a meeting."

These words stunned me but allayed some of my worries. "But what is the difference?" I asked. "Won't union be a result of our meeting?"

"No," answered Jeremiah. "Not yet. You will meet, but not unite, with Verdigris. There is a difference. Union now with Verdigris would separate you forever. But separation would bring about eternal union between you, what that enlightened being known on Terra as the Buddha called Nirvana. This could be the last of your existences. Verdigris is the other half of your soul. At the moment, you are both incomplete, lacking union, and an incomplete soul cannot return to the Cosmic Oversoul to which it belongs. It is vital that you do not fail this test and that you do not incite Verdigris to fail either. Verdigris will always follow the path that you set. Remember that always. You face a great responsibility. If you win this final battle, you will find eternal happiness. If you fail, you will have to start the incarnation cycle once again, from the beginning."

"I do not understand," I cried, feeling the ancient terrors rising again within my being. "How can separation bring unity and unity bring separation? There is no logic to these words!"

The light that swirled around my guides flickered suddenly, and the rays that shone forth blended into the iridescent colors of the rainbow that formed the amphitheater. The two guides seemed to vanish in the blazing multicolored light. Terrified, I withdrew to the farthest point within the light.

"Do not fear," said Joab softly. "You have spoken of logic, a concept that you learned on Terra as Alexander, from your teacher Aristotle. But this logic does not exist in the world of spirit. There is only one truth for the soul, and that truth is union with the Light whence it originated. You incarnate in matter to experience it, and then you return to the Source, or Cosmic Oversoul. That is all. But to return to the Source, you must be purified from contact with matter. If you can accomplish this after one existence, that is perfect bliss, but it is rare. Most of the time, the soul must incarnate several times before it is completely free of corruption. To experience matter fully, it must be divided in two halves, male and female. That is its true essence. To return to the Source, both halves must be purified and unite beforehand. You and Verdigris are the two halves of one soul, and you are about to complete your purification cycle and return to the Light. But you must undergo one final step before that purification is complete. You must overcome matter together, just as you overcame it while apart from each other. That is the final test."

"You were frightened when you saw us blend with the rainbow colors of the Light," interposed Jeremiah. "The rainbow means that there has been a division in the Light; a refraction has divided the colors of the spectrum. This phenomenon is terrestrial; it is caused by the separation in the unity of Light. That is why there is color in the material world. The Light has been divided. Your mission in this last existence will be to unify the Light and in this manner illuminate the human race. To achieve this, you must remain apart from the world and from Verdigris. A union with Verdigris at this time will cause a refraction of your light and a prolonged separation of your essences."

"How can I, so small, bring divine light to the human race?" I asked.

"Remember the teachings of Buddha, which you learned as Chandra?" asked Jeremiah.

"Yes."

"Buddha is one of the great souls who work to bring about the final union of all souls with the Light," said Joab. "His mission on Terra was to bring the lessons of love, kinship, kindness, and compassion to the human race. This universal message is brought not only to Terra but to all the planets in all the galaxies of this Universe by many enlightened souls. One of the most luminous and pure of these beings brought the message of Union and Light to Terra with

the sacrifice of his physical body in a most tragic and igno-
minious death. The message was so powerful that it has
survived the tests of time and matter and still illuminates
the human race. To ensure that it continues to survive, it is
necessary for other souls to sojourn on Terra to brighten
with the purity of their lives the memory of that great soul
and his message of love and sacrifice."

"Is this then my last mission on Terra?" I asked.

"Only if you wish it to be," said Joab. "We have told oftentimes that a soul must accept willingly the missions it is
offered. Free will is one of the most important principles of
Cosmic Law."

"Then I accept," I answered. "But I do not know if I will
be able to resist again the power of matter or delay my
union with Verdigris."

"That is part of the test," said Jeremiah. "We understand
the power of matter, but do not underestimate the power of
your soul or your love for Verdigris. Therein lies your
strength."

"Who was the great soul whose message I must preserve?" I asked curiously.

"His name was Jesus," answered Jeremiah.

Shortly after receiving these instructions, I found myself on Terra once again. This time the voices of Joab and
Jeremiah did not counsel me during my infancy, and I
grew up as a normal child with no memory of the instructions my guides had given me nor of the mission I
had to accomplish.

In contrast to my previous incarnation, my new existence on Terra was surrounded with luxury. I was born this
time into a wealthy family of silk merchants in the country
of Italy. Childhood followed infancy, always surrounded by
whatever my heart would desire. Being of an agreeable and

cheerful disposition, I had many friends who accompanied me in all my childish adventures.

Despite my parents' wealth, I was never accepted by the members of the ruling nobility because of our status as merchants. From an early age, the desire to cover myself with glory on the battlefields obsessed me. It was as if faint echoes of my existence as Alexander still haunted my soul. Driven by this ambition, I joined the army to defend our native city against the threat of invasion by neighboring lords. These were medieval times, and warfare among neighboring cities was the normal way of life.

My first battle proved disastrous. My city was defeated by the invaders, and I was taken prisoner for a year. When I was released, I decided to embark on yet another war expedition, this time to protect the pope against his enemies. But the night before I was to leave on this venture, I had a strange dream in which a voice urged me to return to the city of my birth.

Heeding this dream, I returned to my parents' home. A few days later, walking alongside the road, I arrived at a small chapel, half in ruins, that rose like a little nest among the overgrowth. Captured by the beauty of the place, I entered the chapel. In the semidarkness I could distinguish an old crucifix hanging from one of the walls. The crucifix captured my attention despite the fact that there was nothing unusual about it. When I came closer to examine it, the eyes of the crucified Christ stared directly into mine, and I heard a voice within me say, "My house is in ruins. Repair it!"

Trembling like a leaf, I ran out of the chapel and did not stop until I reached my house. But that night I saw the vision of the crucifix in my dreams, and I heard the same voice, which I now knew to be that of Jesus, repeat the same words: "My house is in ruins. Repair it!"

The next day, recalling the vividness of my dream, I returned to the chapel. This time I felt no fear; if anything, I felt a strange exultation, as if I had found my true destiny. Once in the chapel, I stood again in front of the crucifix.

"My Lord Jesus," I prayed. "If the vision that I have had is not simply a fabrication of my imagination, let me know. I am ready to serve you with all my heart if that is what you wish of me."

Almost instantaneously, I heard the voice of Christ once more, urging me to repair his church. With no doubt in my heart as to the source of the message, I dedicated myself from that day forward to the reconstruction of the chapel. Because I had no money of my own, I took a costly piece of red brocade from my father's warehouse and sold it in one of the neighboring towns. Then I took my bag of gold coins to the chapel and gave it to the ancient priest who attended to it. But the holy man, recognizing me as the son of one of the richest merchants in the area, refused to accept the money.

"This gold belongs to your father, not to you," he said. "It cannot be used to reconstruct the house of God."

"You are right, good father," I said, lowering my head in shame. "I had not thought about that. I will find another way to repair the chapel, without my father's money."

I threw the bag with the money in a corner and stayed to live in the chapel from that moment on. My father, who had by now discovered what I had done, dragged me in front of the ecclesiastical tribunal and demanded the return of his money. The bishop of the city, who knew the reasons why I had sold the cloth, asked me to return the money to my father. Peacefully and without the slightest trace of resentment, I rose and faced the bishop.

"It is true, Excellency," I said. "The money for the bro-cade belongs to my father, and he has the right to ask for it. But this money is not the only thing that belongs to my father. The clothes that I am wearing are also his, and I wish to return them to him as well, because from this day on-ward I only recognize God as my father."

As I spoke, I began to remove all of my clothes until I stood completely naked in front of my father and the eccle-siastical tribunal. I then deposited the clothes and the bag of coins at my father's feet. My father's face drained of color, and he shook visibly with ill-contained rage as the bishop covered my naked body with his mantle.

Once outside the tribunal, one of the gardeners gave me a sackcloth, from which I made a makeshift robe marked with a white cross to show my dedication to Jesus. I then tied a rope around my waist, and this, along with a pair of sandals and a hood also made of sackcloth, became from that moment on my entire wardrobe. Recalling the poverty of Jesus and his exhortation to his apostles to live off the charity of others, I embraced poverty as the most beautiful of brides.

I had not forgotten the promise I made to Jesus to re-construct the chapel. I began to beg on corners for stones, bricks, and mortar with which to accomplish the task. My total devotion to this cause attracted other kindred souls who also desired to give themselves to God, and soon we became a small band of missionaries dedicated to peace and goodwill. Using our combined strengths, we worked day and night until we finally raised again the small chapel, which came to be known as the Church of St. Damian.

How sweet were those days for me and how full of love for Christ and faith in the Creator! Other churches were re-constructed by our small band after this, and we began calling ourselves the "Friars Minor," or little brothers, to underline our unworthiness. But despite my great adoration of Jesus and his church, I was never ordained as a priest, and when I went to Rome with my friars years later to ask recognition from the Pope, I was surprised to learn that he had already heard of us.

When at last we returned to our native city of Assisi, I was asked by the bishop to give a sermon at the cathedral. That evening, after speaking fervently on the merits of poverty and the love of Christ, one of my friars told me that the daughter of one of the most powerful nobles of the city wanted to talk to me. I readily agreed to see her, because nothing pleased me more than to spread the word of Christ to the rich and powerful and to help them realize the futility of earthly riches.

A few minutes later, the friar returned, accompanied by a beautiful young woman no more than eighteen years of age, dressed with all the pomp and luxury of her class. I arose to receive her and extended my hand to the one stretched out before me, but I did not get to touch her. A blinding light came between us, and I suddenly heard an echo that surrounded me like a vortex of fire.

"Verdigris!" it cried. "Verdigris!"

Like a frozen marble statue, I stood before her, my extended hand mere inches from her own.

"Father Francis," whispered the friar in my ear. "This is the Lady Claire I was telling you about."

§

after death

what happens

separation

what happens

after death

9 HOW CAN I DESCRIBE THE
moment when I found myself once more face to
face with Verdigris? In her beloved presence, I regained the memory of all my previous existences
and the instructions of my guides. Separation,
they had said, is vital for total union. But how
could I endure another separation from the other
half of my soul?

Having regained my cosmic memory, I knew
that the personality of Francis of Assisi was simply a disguise behind which my spirit lay hidden,
a transient existence in the infinity of the cosmos. Of what importance was this life? Why did I
have to sacrifice my union with Verdigris in order
to live out this obscure existence?

"Because of Jesus," said Verdigris, speaking
through the lips of Claire of Assisi. Her trembling
hand found mine, and her heavenly eyes told me
that she too had recognized me.

"What did you say, my lady?" asked the friar,
surprised at her words.

Claire turned her blue eyes toward him.

"Because of Jesus," she repeated, "I have come
to see Father Francis. Because of Jesus I have decided to dedicate my life to poverty and sacrifice."

The friar looked at her curiously. He knew
that she was the eldest daughter of the Offre-
duccis, one of the most noble and powerful families in Assisi. And yet this exquisite creature, the

most beautiful flower in the house of Offreducci, wanted to abandon the splendor of her father's house to follow in the steps of Christ.

"And what does your family say about your decision, my lady?" he asked, discreetly observing the richness of her elegant brocaded gown.

"I have not yet told them of my plans," she answered softly, looking at me all the while. "I want Father Francis to decide my destiny. I will do whatever he says."

My spirit rebelled within me. Why did I have to make the awesome decision? Why was this terrible responsibility to be mine alone?

"Because you are the weakest," came Joab's answer from across the cosmos. "The responsibility will make you stronger."

"Because of Jesus," Claire repeated, withdrawing her hand from mine.

Then suddenly, like a great awakening, the memory of the chapel and the crucifix with its transfixing eyes and the voice of Jesus imploring me to repair his church came rushing to my mind. It was for the sake of Jesus that I had to live this life of sacrifice and separation. It was for love of him and to keep alive the memory of his sacrifice and his message that I had to endure this bitter separation. My mission this time on Terra was to solidify the teachings of Buddha and Jesus into One. Mine was to be a life of poverty and continuous sacrifice, like the lives of these two great teachers. It was my mission to remind humanity that not only human beings but all creatures in nature are equal, that the cosmos is our soul and the material world just an illusion. In order to show humanity that the physical body was transitory, it was necessary for me to reject all worldly pleasures, including the love of Verdigris, not so that the world would follow my example, but rather to show them through my example that the body and the things of the earth all pass, and that only the spirit endures forever. The salvation of the world was locked in this simple yet profound teaching. I understood then the importance of my mission and the necessity of a physical separation from Verdigris. What did the sacrifice of one life on Terra mean when compared with the eternal life of our soul?

"For Jesus," I said, looking directly at Claire of Assisi. "If you are willing, I will tell you how to serve God and him."

A dazzling smile illuminated her beloved face.

"I am willing," she answered. Her eyes told me she had understood my decision.

That very night Claire abandoned her home in secret and prepared to meet me and my friars at the Church of the Angels. Before the altar and in the presence of the monks, she vowed her service to Christ and changed her beautiful robes for the sackcloth and sandals that were to be her only dress. She never returned to her father's palace, spending the rest of her life in absolute poverty behind the walls of a cloister with other women who, like herself, had dedicated themselves to the service of God. But it was she, Claire of Assisi, whom the world remembered as one of the purest souls that ever inhabited the third planet of Solaris.

During the next fifteen years, I carried the banner of my faith everywhere I went. My small band of friars grew like seeds planted in fertile ground, extending by example the love of Christ and the merits of a humble life to the four corners of the world. Despite the fact that one of the main rules of our order was the renunciation of material wealth and begging for our food and needs, thousands of young men joined our ranks from every social order.

My dedication to the teachings of Christ grew with the years. His great humility and acceptance of the divine will were the most valuable lessons I learned on Terra. Through him I learned that we must never allow our bodies to dominate our spirits and that no matter how long our time on earth may seem, it is but a grain of sand when compared to the eternity of the soul. That was why Jesus was able to resist such terrible temptations. He knew that their duration was momentary and that pain was as illusory as pleasure. By exerting complete control over the material world, he gained power over it. All the miracles he accomplished were natural because he understood the cosmos and its laws.

As soon as I understood these things, I immersed myself in the study of nature. The sun and moon, the earth and sky, the rivers and the seas, for me they were all the expression of God the Creator. They were all my brothers and sisters because Terra was part of a force that was both unifying and unique. When this concept of Universal Oneness illuminated my mind, I was able to perform the same transformations that Jesus did. My spirit so identified with him that my hands and my feet began to exhibit the stigmata he suffered in his martyrdom.

For the friars, the stigmata were a sign of my sanctification. But in reality they were nothing more than my total identification with Jesus.

My life on Terra as Francis of Assisi was the happiest and most complete of all my existences. Verdigris was always with me in spirit, despite of being physically apart.

The end of my life came unexpectedly, like the blowing out of a candle. When I finally let go of the yoke of life, I gave thanks to the Cosmic Oversoul for the gift of this last lifetime and the eternal one to come. Filled with serene happiness, I asked my friars to carry me to Claire's convent. When we were again face to face, her eyes, full of light, embraced me with the immensity of her eternal love.

"We have overcome!" whispered my soul.

"For Jesus," she answered.

§

after death

what happens

union

what happens

after death

10 So INSIGNIFICANT IS THE CON-
cept of time in comparison to the eternity of the
spirit that although I left Terra twenty-seven
years before Verdigris, we arrived before Jeremiah
and Joab at the same time.

The joy that radiated from our beloved guides
was greater even than our own.

"How very long you had to wait and how
many lives you had to live before you could meet
again on the threshold of eternity!" exclaimed
Jeremiah.

"I understand now that it was necessary," I
said, my soul filled with great serenity. "There
was much I had to learn, and much that had to
be purified in me before I could find the truth."

"What is the truth?" asked Joab, his luminous
aura shimmering softly.

"The unification of all things," I answered.
"There is only one truth, but an infinity of manifestations."

"Do you know who you are?" asked Jeremiah.

"I am the soul of the Universe, the atom from
which all is created," I answered.

"Who is Verdigris?" asked Joab.

"I am Verdigris," I said.

"Where was she all these millennia?" the guide
persisted.

"She was always with me," I answered. "But I
was so entrenched in matter that I could never
perceive her. It was in Assisi where I was finally

227

able to recognize her. But to achieve it, Verdigris had to separate from me for the first time. Only through this separation was I able to perceive her essence."

"The Light is finally in you," said the guides. "At last you are One."

All the splendid colors of the rainbow that formed the amphitheater where we found ourselves fused together in a blinding flash of dazzling white light. I felt myself being pulled into the center of this Light, and suddenly I *was* the Light. My spirit extended itself into the infinite in a wave of indescribable love and at the same time contracted into the core of the atom, which is the foundation of the Universe. For a miraculous instant, I felt Verdigris palpitate within me before our souls fused for all eternity. A rapturous, endless bliss inundated my being.

My purified soul ascended rapidly to the center of the Universe to unite with the Cosmic Oversoul that is the Source of all that exists. The Light, brighter and whiter than a million suns, illuminated the cosmos in a boundless fountain of gamma rays and others as yet unknown in Terra, so bright as to be unperceived by human eyes. At its core, in concentric circles of crystalline fire, the most sublime souls who had found bliss through love and sacrifice basked eternally in the glorious Light of the Creator. Among them I recognized the shining soul of Buddha and the majestic glory of Jesus.

Upon arriving at this place of celestial beauty, my soul immediately united with these souls in eternal joy. Perfect awareness within the Light that was the Creator welcomed me with infinite tenderness. How can I describe that ineffable feeling? How do I express the inexpressible?

"Kirkudian, are you happy at last?" whispered Joab to my soul.

"Infinitely," I answered.

"Come with me then, so you can see other planes of existence where no such happiness exists."

Rapidly we descended to the internal planes of the astral world. Behind us we left the eternal bliss that Buddha called Nirvana. Around us, the Light began to fade and diffract into thousands of strange colors I had never seen before. As we continued to descend, I saw that each plane was different, as were their inhabitants. The higher planes had souls that were evolved but not yet integrated into the Light. They had only an intellectual awareness of their existence without recognizing the presence of the spirit.

The inferior planes were inhabited by unhappy souls full of destructive and adverse sentiments. The Light was so dim there that it absorbed nearly all of our own. How many cries of anguish and desperation we heard in these shadowy areas! How my spirit suffered in the face of such tragic spiritual disintegration!

"Why have you brought me here?" I asked at last, horrified. "I cannot withstand such destruction."

"Because you are still a young soul," said Joab. "You have barely completed your integration with the Source. We took you to the Light so you could feel its presence and bask in its love. The Light is home to you. It is what you are. But it is important that you learn to use that Light to illuminate those in darkness and to guide the ones who are searching for the truth. Whenever you need to replenish your light or desire to reunite with the Source, you can ascend to the Creator. But then you must return to continue your work. That is the common goal of every evolved soul, and it will remain so until total unification has been completed."

"In what way can I help?" I asked eagerly.

"By serving as a teacher, guiding whoever may need you, giving hope to those who have lost it and inspiration to those who are seekers on the path."

"Here?" I asked.

"Here or wherever you wish," replied Joab. "You can choose to do your work in any area of the Universe. If you wish, you can return as a guide to any of the planets in which you lived, or you can go to places you have never visited. It is you who must decide, as always."

"If I may, then, I would like to choose Terra," I said without hesitation. "It was there where I most suffered and where I finally found myself."

"Terra is a planet greatly afflicted," responded Joab. "Its evolution is rapid and dangerous. You can do a great deal of good there. Perhaps as a messenger of sorrow, since you have suffered so much. Along with pain, you can bring hope and consolation to humanity. Would you like this mission?"

"No," I responded quickly. "Sorrow is not a good friend to me. I wish to bring it to no one."

"Sorrow is necessary for the evolution of the soul," said Joab gravely. "You cannot ignore or reject it."

"It is not my intention to reject it," I said quickly. "But you said that I was free to choose . . . "

"Yes, you are," said Joab gently. "Is there something else you would rather do? How about inspiration?"

"Inspiration," I pondered. "Yes. That would be a perfect mission. I could help humanity by inspiring them to rise above their weaknesses and all obstacles and guide them on the path to the Light."

"So be it," said Joab. "From this moment onward, that will be your mission on Terra. No one will tell you who the souls are whom you are to help. That will be your decision. But choose well," he warned, "and do justice to your mission so that humanity will advance swiftly to the Light."

Many years have passed since I began my mission on Terra. I have already told you the story of the first life I transformed through inspiration, the Russian ballerina named Anna Pavlova. After I completed my mission with her, I worked with many others to help them fulfill their dreams and further their evolution. Some of these lives were already highly evolved, while others were neophytes on the evolutionary path, but I gave them all the faith and perseverance they needed to achieve their aims. The humblest soul I guided was that of a beggar whom I helped transcend his tragic situation. Through my constant prodding, he persevered, found his way back to human society, and became a highly respected and beloved teacher; but most importantly, he evolved into a spirit of great vision and Light. Among the more evolved souls, there was a nuclear physicist named Albert Einstein, whom I helped unravel the mysteries of Light, and a Hindu lawyer named Mohandas Gandhi, whom I taught that God is identical with Truth and that He Is, even though the world may deny Him. These teachings he passed on to the rest of humanity, thus furthering human faith and evolution. These two were easy to inspire because they were spirits of great faith and generosity.

I am still here, from the Himalayas to the Mediterranean, in the northern and southern latitudes and the eastern and western longitudes of Terra. My exalted spirit extends itself like a protective mantle throughout the length and breadth of the planet. If you need me, call me. I am here to guide you. My light will illuminate your soul whenever you are in doubt or in need of guidance. Do not forget my name. I am Kirkudian.

§

bibliography

Aristotle. *Metaphysics.* Trans. R. Hope. New York, 1952.

Barth, G. F. *Nova Yoga.* New York, 1974.

Bernstein, M. *The Search for Bridey Murphy.* New York, 1971.

Besant, A., and C. W. Leadbeater. *Thought Forms.* Wheaton, Ill., 1925.

Blavatsky, H. P. *The Secret Doctrine.* London, 1965.

Boehme, J. *The Signature of All Things.* London, 1969.

Boss, A. P. "Companions to Young Stars." *Scientific American* 273, no. 4 (October 1995): 134.

Brennan, J. H. *Astral Doorways.* New York, 1971.

Brierley, J. *The Thinking Machine.* New Jersey, 1973.

Brown, R. *Unfinished Symphonies: Voices from Beyond.* New York, 1971.

Capra, F. *The Tao of Physics.* Boulder, Colo., 1975.

Thomas of Celano. *First and Second Life of St Francis* (thirteenth-century biography). Trans. P. Hermann. London, 1963.

Churchland, P. M. *Matter and Consciousness.* Cambridge, Mass., 1988.

Crick, F. *The Astonishing Hypothesis.* New York, 1994.

Darwin, C. R. *The Origin of Species.* London, 1976.

Davidson, G. A. *Dictionary of Angels.* New York, 1971.

Davies, P. *God and the New Physics.* New York, 1983.
———. *The Mind of God.* New York, 1992.

Davies, P., and J. Gribbin. *The Matter Myth.* New York, 1992.

Dennett, D. C. *Consciousness Explained.* Boston, 1991.

232

De Reuck, A., and J. Knight, eds. *Caste and Race.* New York, 1964.

Dimmitt, C., and J. A. B. van Buitenen, eds. *Classical Hindu Mythology.* Philadelphia, 1978.

Dumont, L. *Homo Hierarchicus: The Caste System and Its Implications.* New York, 1970.

Eadie, B. J. *Embraced by the Light.* Placerville, Calif., 1992.

Einstein, A. *Ideas and Opinions.* New York, 1954.

———. *Relativity, The Special and the General Theory.* New York, 1961.

———. *The World As I See It.* New York, 1949.

Feynman, R. "Mathematical Formulation of the Quantum Theory of Electromagnetic Interaction." *Selected Papers of Quantum Electrodynamics* (1958): 272.

Gamow, G. *The Creation of the Universe.* New York, 1973.

Garrett, E. *Telepathy.* New York, 1968.

———. *Adventures in the Supernatural.* New York, 1967.

Gleick, J. *Chaos.* New York, 1987.

González-Wippler, M. *Santería: The Religion.* St. Paul, Minn., 1994.

Green, P. *Alexander the Great* (with genealogy). London, 1970.

Hapgood, C. H. *Voices of Spirit: Through the Psychic Experience of Elwood Babbitt.* New York, 1975.

Hawking, S. *A Brief History of Time.* New York, 1988.

———. *Black Holes and Baby Universes.* New York, 1993.

Hayes, C. J. H., and J. H. Hanscom. *Ancient Civilizations: Mainstreams of Civilization.* Vol. 1. New York, 1968.

Heisenberg, W. *Physics and Beyond.* New York, 1971.

Hopper, R. J. *The Early Greeks.* New York, 1976.

Hoyle, F. *Astronomy and Cosmology: A Modern Course.* New York, 1975.

Huxley, A. *A Perennial Philosophy.* New York, 1962.

Jacolliot, L. *Occult Science in India and among the Ancients.* New York, 1971.

Jahn, R. J., and B. J. Dunne. *Margins of Reality: The Role of Consciousness in the Physical World.* New York, 1987.

———. "On the Quantum Mechanics of Consciousness, with Application to Anomalous Phenomena." *Foundations of Physics* 16, no. 8 (1986).

Jastrow, R. *God and the Astronomers.* New York, 1977.

Jeans, J. *The Mysterious Universe.* New York, 1948.

Jung, C. G. *The Archetypes of the Collective Unconscious.* New York, 1959.

——. *The Structure and Dynamics of the Psyche.* New York, 1960.

——. *Mysterium Coniunctionis.* New York, 1963.

Jung, C. G., and W. Pauli. *The Interpretation of Nature and the Psyche* (Bollingen series LI). Princeton, N.J., 1955.

Kaku, M. *Hyperspace.* Oxford, 1994.

Kant, I. *Prolegomena to Any Future Metaphysics.* New York, 1951.

Kardec, A. *The Book of Spirits.* New York, 1982.

——. *The Book of Mediums.* New York, 1970.

Kent, E. W. *The Brains of Men and Machines.* New York, 1981.

Kilner, W. J. *The Aura.* London, 1911.

Kosslyn, S. M. *Image and Brain.* Cambridge, Mass., 1994.

Kubler-Ross, Elizabeth. *On Life after Death.* Berkeley, Calif., 1991.

Kung, H. *Eternal Life? Life after Death as a Medical, Philosophical and Theological Problem.* New York, 1984.

Leadbeater, C. W. *The Chakras.* Wheaton, Ill., 1985.

——. *Man Visible and Invisible.* Wheaton, Ill., 1980.

Leibniz, W. *Monadology.* London, 1890.

Leslie, J. *Universes.* London, 1989.

Lund, D. H. *Death and Consciousness.* Jefferson, N.C., 1985.

Lycan, W. G. *Consciousness.* Cambridge, Mass., 1984.

Maimonides, M. *The Guide to the Perplexed.* New York, 1956.

McDougall, W. *Outline of Abnormal Psychology.* New York, 1926.

Moody, R. *Life after Life.* Harrisburg, PA, 1976.

Monroe, R. A. *Journeys Out of the Body.* New York, 1971.

Montgomery, R. *Threshold to Tomorrow.* New York, 1982.

Murchie, G. *Music of the Spheres.* New York, 1961.

Ornstein, R., ed. *The Nature of Human Consciousness.* New York, 1974.

Ostrander, S. and L. Schroeder. *PSI, Psychic Discoveries behind the Iron Curtain.* London, 1973.

Ouspensky, P. *Tertium Organum: A Key to the Enigmas of the Universe.* New York, 1968.

Panchadasi, Swami. *The Astral World.* New York, 1972.

Papus. *Reincarnation.* New York, 1991.

Penfield, W. *The Mystery of the Mind.* Princeton, N.J., 1975.

Penrose, R. *The Emperor's New Mind.* New York, 1989.

———. *Shadows of the Mind.* Oxford, 1994.

Perez y Mena, A. *Speaking With the Dead.* New York, 1991.

Plato. *Phaedo.* New York, 1942.

Popper, K., and J. C. Eccles. *The Self and Its Brain.* Berlin, 1977.

Powell, A. E. *The Astral Body.* Wheaton, Ill., 1982.

Progoff, I. *Jung, Synchronicity and Human Destiny.* New York, 1973.

Reanney, D. *After Death.* New York, 1991.

Renault, M. *The Nature of Alexander.* New York, 1975.

Rhine, J. B. *Extrasensory Perception.* Boston, Mass.,1934.

de Riencourt, A. *The Eye of Shiva: Eastern Mysticism and Science.* New York, 1980.

Rinpoche, S. *The Tibetan Book of Living and Dying.* San Francisco, 1992.

Rose, S. *The Conscious Brain.* New York, 1976.

———. *The Making of Memory, From Molecules to Mind.* New York, 1992.

Russell, B. *The ABC of Relativity.* London, 1958.

———. *The Analysis of Mind.* London, 1921.

Sagan, C. *The Cosmic Connection.* New York, 1973.

Schrödinger, E. *What Is Life?* London, 1969.

Sheldrake, R. *A New Science of Life.* Los Angeles, 1981.

Shipman, H. I. *Black Holes, Quasars and the Universe.* Boston, Mass., 1976.

Smoot, G., and K. Davidson. *Wrinkles in Time.* New York, 1994.

Sneath, P. H. A. *Planets and Life.* London, 1970.

Stevenson, I. *Twenty Cases Suggestive of Reincarnation.* New York, 1971.

Thomas, E. J. *The Life of Buddha.* London, 1927.

Thorne, K. S. *Black Holes and Time Warps.* New York, 1994.

Tipler, F. J. *The Physics of Immortality.* New York, 1994.

Younger, P. *Introduction to Indian Religious Thought.* Philadelphia, 1972.

Zukov, G. *The Dancing Wu Li Masters.* New York, 1979.

index

Stay in Touch . . .

Llewellyn publishes hundreds of books on your favorite subjects

On the following pages you will find listed some books now available on related subjects. Your local bookstore stocks most of these and will stock new Llewellyn titles as they become available. We urge your patronage.

Order by Phone

Call toll-free within the U.S. and Canada, 1-800-THE MOON.
In Minnesota call (612) 291-1970.
We accept Visa, MasterCard, and American Express.

Order by Mail

Send the full price of your order (MN residents add 7% sales tax) in U.S. funds to:

> Llewellyn Worldwide
> P.O. Box 64383, Dept. K327-1
> St. Paul, MN 55164-0383, U.S.A.

Postage and Handling

- ◆ $4.00 for orders $15.00 and under
- ◆ $5.00 for orders over $15.00
- ◆ No charge for orders over $100.00

We ship UPS in the continental United States. We cannot ship to P.O. boxes. Orders shipped to Alaska, Hawaii, Canada, Mexico, and Puerto Rico will be sent first-class mail.
International orders: Airmail—add freight equal to price of each book to the total price of order, plus $5.00 for each non-book item (audio-tapes, etc.). Surface mail—Add $1.00 per item.
Allow 4–6 weeks delivery on all orders. Postage and handling rates subject to change.

Group Discounts

We offer a 20% quantity discount to group leaders or agents. You must order a minimum of 5 copies of the same book to get our special quantity price.

Free Catalog

Get a free copy of our color catalog, *New Worlds of Mind and Spirit.* Subscribe for just $10.00 in the United States and Canada ($20.00 overseas, first-class mail). Many bookstores carry *New Worlds*—ask for it!